It Takes A Village To Raise A Criminal!
5 Ugly Facts™
About Institutionalized
Human Behavior
(A Human Behavior Guide for Everyday Humans)

You are Needed to Raise
a Successful Village!!
Thank You!! Dr. Jenn

Dr. Jennifer L. Rounds-Bryant

Publisher
Mental Health Solutions
P.O. Box 14413
Research Triangle Park, NC 27709-4413
www.5UglyFacts.com

First Edition
First Printing

Printed in the United States of America

ISBN-13: 978-0-9798600-1-0
ISBN-10: 0-9798600-1-6

Library of Congress Control Number: 2008932334

Dedication

This second book is also dedicated to my children, Jillian and Emmanuel, who are being guided responsibly through childhood by our village. My priceless network of parents, family, and friends – *you know who you are darlings* – share equally in the dedication because you are important members of our village.

Acknowledgements

The seeds of the *5 Ugly Facts*^{TM} book series were planted 18 years ago when I decided that everybody should have the information that social scientists have known about human behavior for decades. This book is the second in the series which serves as the vehicle for making behavioral facts easily accessible to students, professionals, and everyday people.

Early Support for the Second Book

A great big thank you goes out to the people who purchased copies of the book before it went to press. I will always be grateful for the inspiration inspired by your tangible show of support!

Ongoing Support for the Book Series

I would like to thank those who purchased the first book (**Men Don't Like Kids!**) and gave amazing feedback about it. Many thanks also go to those who gave suggestions about topics for future books. As always, members of my network of family and friends continue to nurture the development of the book series with generous amounts of support and encouragement.

Book Publishing Team

Writing and publishing this second book was made so much easier by the wonderful book publishing team established during the publishing of the first book. It is my grand dream that I will someday be able to pay retail prices for the assistance provided by members of my team. Until then, I am grateful to each one for taking the time to do one more thing for me.

Some of the many human service professionals in my network reviewed each *Ugly Fact* to ensure that it was quick and easy to read and error-free. Dr. Jack Monell, Ms. Kesha Lee, Dr. Sheara Williams, Dr. Andre´ Stevenson, Dr. Penny McKenzie, Dr. M. Lela Demby, Mr. Clinton Dubose, and Dr. Patrick Flynn served as the review team.

Ms. Elnora Shields served as editor and Ms. Danisa Baker served as copy-editor for the entire book. Mr. Michael Slaughter provided graphic design for the book cover, along with many other forms of professional guidance.

Table Of Contents

Introduction:
The Set-Up

The Take-Home Message

1. This book translates decades of research about institutionalized human behavior into everyday language for everyday people.

2. Individuals, families, and peers play important roles in juvenile delinquency.

3. Indeed, it takes a village to raise a criminal: education, child welfare, mental health, juvenile justice, and religion.

Purpose of the Book

Translation of Research

The purpose of this book is to translate decades of research that details how five human service systems - education, child welfare, mental health, criminal justice, and religious - work individually and collectively to continually deliver to the United States criminal justice system more criminals than it can safely house at any one time, accounting for the highest rate of incarceration in the industrialized world.[1] The United States criminal justice system is an industry that has enjoyed 33 years of continuous growth, coinciding with the 30-year history of testing-based education reform.[1,2]

Growing Criminals

In order to keep growing, the system must take in more and more criminals. Since criminals are rarely imported from other countries for incarceration purposes, then that means that America must grow her own criminals. The village complies quite efficiently in supplying this ever-increasing demand.

The Role of the Village

The village raises a child and a criminal in much the same way. What determines whether a person becomes a criminal, a superstar, or an average Joe is the village's response to the person during childhood. The extent to which the village responds to a child like she will become a criminal, a superstar, or an average Jo plays a large part in determining which of these she will become. A child's experiences with her family and in her community environment play important roles in her eventual outcome, which is well-known. Not-so-well-known is the hand that the education, child welfare, mental health, criminal justice, and religious systems have in raising criminals.

Maximizing the Positive

Before taking a close look at the roles of the five selected human service systems in raising criminals, the roles of biological and individual characteristics, parents, and peers will be reviewed in order to provide a basic understanding of these micro-level factors, within the context of the discussion of the macro-level systems. The goal of "**It Takes A Village to Raise A Criminal**" is to help everyday people to understand what criminal justice scholars and human service professionals have known for decades. The bonus goal is for readers to identify new ways to move the village towards maximizing the positive outcomes for all of its members, and away from the deliberate marginalization of some of its members.

The Picture Of Criminality

What Is a Criminal?

A crime is an unlawful act. A criminal is a person who commits unlawful acts, whether or not he is ever caught or punished. Criminal behavior ranges from violent and non-violent juvenile offenses to minor adult infractions and violent adult crimes. Most children who commit status offenses (e.g., behaviors that are illegal only for children such as curfew violations) and minor crimes (e.g., petty shoplifting) do not go on to a life of adult crime. Likewise, most adults who engage in minor infractions such as violating speed limits, cheating on their taxes, or stealing cable television do not end up as chronically-incarcerated criminals. However, the chronically-incarcerated adult criminal does not just appear out of nowhere.[3]

The Road to Criminality

A person usually grows into an adult criminal in a very predictable way, over a significant period of time, usually beginning in early childhood. Children who are not easily comforted, restless, and/or prone to take risks are easily identified in families as the super cranky baby and the wild child, in church as the child who just will not sit still and listen, in pre-school as the child who bullies the other children and will not sit still long enough to learn his letters, and in the neighborhood as the elementary school child who roams around when other children have long since disappeared indoors. With the proper set of circumstances, these children will go on to engage in increasingly inappropriate behaviors like mouthing off at their parents, throwing chairs in the classroom, and being suspended from school. Before long, a child like this skips school, shoplifts, tries cigarettes and alcohol, and finds other kids like him to hang around with, all before leaving elementary school.[3]

As he leaves elementary school and moves into intermediate and high school, he continues to engage in increasingly delinquent behavior. These include regularly missing school, violating established curfew laws for minors, regular substance use, shoplifting, and even breaking and entering. With increased exposure to agents of the juvenile justice system, he typically begins a long and enduring journey as a bon-a-fide convicted criminal. This journey usually begins first with incarceration in the juvenile justice system, then as an adult in the criminal justice system.[3]

Individual Factors Related To Criminal Behavior

The Role of Biology and Personality

This description of the early behavior signs which populate the road to criminality places emphasis on innate characteristics of the child. For example, restlessness, fussiness, and risk-taking are often associated with temperament – characteristics with which children are born that serve as the building blocks of personality style. Further, challenging personality styles (being self-centered, rebellious, and/or non-conforming) can lead to difficulty with self-control, which is also an important precursor to criminality. Finally, behavior disorders such as Attention Deficit Hyperactivity and Conduct disorder, as well as exposure to drugs and alcohol during fetal development have been associated with later criminal behavior.[3]

Yet, even these early signs which are often associated with criminality are subject to the influences of the village. The baby with the difficult temperament can be taught to self-soothe, the restless child can be taught to quietly entertain himself, and the risk-taking child can be guided towards more socially-accepted challenges before these propensities develop into self-control problems.[3]

Even after the child begins to exhibit serious self-control problems, the right set of circumstances can help to transform the child into one who conforms to enough pro-social behaviors to steer clear of the path to criminality. The village's response to children with these characteristics determines whether they travel down the road of conventionality or ride the slippery slope to a lifetime of criminality.[1]

Primary Social Environment & Criminal Behavior

Social Learning Theory

The social environment plays a primary role in the development of criminal behavior. In fact, Social Learning Theory states that criminal behavior is learned from a person's social environment, of which parents and peers are core elements. A person's perspective of crime is typically shaped by what he experiences in his immediate environment (e.g., family and community). If he grows up seeing criminal behavior as normal, then it is reasonable to believe that he will see criminal behavior as normal, and not necessarily as a deviant behavior that requires him to make a special appraisal of right and wrong before deciding whether to engage in the behavior or not.[3]

However, Social Learning Theory states that learning about criminal behavior does not necessarily lead to a life of crime for most children who are reared in crime-ridden social environments. In order to increase the possibility that exposure to criminal social environments will lead to criminal behavior, criminal behavior must be modeled by those whom children regard as good role models (e.g., parents and other trusted adults), the perceived benefits must outweigh the perceived consequences, and there must be opportunities for practicing the behavior (e.g., with peers).[3]

Parenting & Criminal Behavior

Outside of the individual himself, parents are seen as the most influential source of criminal behavior. The impact of parents on criminal behavior is well-studied. Research indicates that lack of supervision, harsh and inconsistent discipline, and parental role-modeling of criminal behavior play important roles in the development of criminal behavior in children.

Lack of Supervision. Many parents rejoice when their children become old enough to take care of themselves. For a number of reasons, the age at which parents view their children as capable of self-care varies from household to household. Many parents work several jobs, and may deem their children as independent as early as 7 or 8 years old so that they do not have to pay for child care. Others may wait until their children are teens before they begin to leave them unsupervised for long periods of time. In either case, unsupervised children are free to come under the influences of whatever and whoever is in their environment. The extent to which the environment is populated by criminal behavior increases the likelihood that unsupervised children will make their way toward the negative influences, especially if there is a lack of positive alternatives such as vocational or sports activities.[3]

Harsh and Inconsistent Discipline. Discipline can be a tricky thing for many parents. Effective discipline requires more thought than most parents realize or have time to give. Standard parenting guidelines for disciplining children underscore the need for clear and consistent rules regarding expected behavior, along with reasonable and consistent responses to rule violations. Research indicates that parents who ignore most of their children's negative behavior, but then respond randomly and harshly (stinging insults or prolonged spankings) to some negative behavior interfere with their child's ability to discern the difference between right and wrong. Further, the child perceives the usual permissiveness as neglectful and the harsh discipline as abusive. The end result of harsh and inconsistent discipline is a child who has an insecure attachment to his parents and does not understand the basic rules for self-control.[3]

Parental Role – Modeling. Parents provide children with the most important example of how to behave. If they engage in positive, predictable, and consistent behavior, then children learn to engage in the same behaviors. Likewise, if parents' behaviors are negative, unpredictable, and inconsistent, then their children will learn the same things. Research indicates that having a parent in prison is an important predictor of future incarceration for children. In addition, witnessing domestic violence between parents and being victims of abuse at the hands of parents are especially powerful examples of parental role-modeling that many criminals experience in their childhoods.[3] Lest we forget, the modeling of more common forms of adult criminal behavior (such as having parents who defraud the government, cable companies, or their places of employment) also communicates to children powerful messages about the importance of obeying laws.

Negative Peers & Criminal Behavior

Negative Peer Influences. Research traces the path that children take to association with delinquent peers. It begins with difficulty following basic rules and frequent isolation from positive peers (e.g., discipline involving sitting out of play time and suspension from school). Eventually, children with behavior problems will find like others. Associating with negative peers allows for the group identity and acceptance that all children desire, along with the opportunity to practice negative behavior with group support. Negative peer associations often include gang activity, but this is not always the case. Small groups of negative peers often support each other without formal involvement with youth gangs. In addition, individuals can associate with gang members without formally joining a gang.[3]

Youth Gangs. The motivation and consequences for involvement in youth gangs are well documented. Children with early behavior problems, school failure, and delinquency are the perfect candidates for gang membership by age 15.[3] Intervention at any of these points goes a long way in stemming the long-term consequences of even short periods of gang involvement: increased serious and violent criminal behavior and decreased exposure to mainstream values and opportunities.[3]

Negative Peers are Everywhere. Although unsupervised children tend to have more access to negative peers who are in their social environments, coming under the influence of negative peers is not the exclusive domain of unsupervised children. Negative peers can be found in any environment, and therefore serve as a special challenge to address. For example, peers who smoke, drink, use and sell drugs, buy and sell term papers, and engage in all sorts of criminal behavior can be found in education, sports, and social club settings of all types. So, the notion that only "at-risk" children are in danger of associating with negative peers is a closely held myth.[3]

It Takes A Village To Raise A Criminal

The Role of the Village

The idea that it takes a village to raise a criminal goes squarely against what most people think about the traditional role of the village. The notion is that there are human service systems in place in the village to help people, and indeed there are and they do. However, the *Ugly Fact* is that the very systems that help some people with their basic needs turn right around and do a disservice to many of the people who seek their services. Both the help and the hurt are knowingly and unknowingly handed out in a predictable manner by the professionals working in these systems. These systems operate according to such a well-oiled and ingrained template that the actual professionals and consumers are interchangeable with respect to achieving the predictable outcomes.

The tenets of the basic criminology theories are demonstrated regularly in the human service systems that play a role in raising criminals: education, child welfare, mental health, juvenile justice, and religion. To be sure, primary family and social systems are not to be overlooked in the constellation of variables which impact the likelihood that a child will grow up to be a criminal. However, it is quite misleading to repeatedly highlight these micro-level variables without considering the macro-level influences of the human service systems that operate individually and collectively to consistently raise criminals.

The American Education System

Arguably the most important macro-level system in the lives of children is the American education system, including public, private, religious, and any other institutional education setting. The primary purpose of the American education system is to equip most children to grow into working class adults with the minimal basic education required to meet the needs of the prevailing American industries.[4] When the education system fails in this process, as it manages to do in so many creative ways, then the children who are deliberately left behind are the prime candidates for the criminal justice system.

The American Child Welfare System

The core responsibility of the American child welfare system is to ensure that children's basic needs are met. These needs include shelter, food, clothing, and safety.[5] Children who find themselves in need of child welfare services often fare poorly on a number of levels. If their mothers are dependent upon welfare, they are typically among the poorest Americans.[6] Among children who find themselves in the custody of the child welfare system due to insufficient and/or harmful parenting, their fate is dubious at best. Foster care is often associated with little familial attachment and multiple movements.[7] This lifestyle is associated with problem behaviors and criminal justice system involvement.

The American Mental Health System

Mental illness, including addiction, is associated with a myriad of familial and environmental challenges which support the raising of criminals. For example, parents with mental health and addiction problems are more likely to have difficulty providing the safe, predictable, stimulating environment that children need to acquire developmentally-appropriate skills. Similarly, children suffering from mental disorders such as attention deficit hyperactivity disorder, conduct disorder, substance abuse and dependence, depression, and anxiety disorders also have a difficult time learning appropriate coping and self-control skills. Children impacted by unmanaged adult and/or personal mental illness are therefore in jeopardy of being set on a trajectory of school failure and subsequent involvement in the child welfare, mental health, and criminal justice systems.[8]

There is long-standing stigma about mental illness in America, so the average response to mental illness is denial and secrecy, instead of treatment. When crazy behavior can no longer be kept secret, because of child maltreatment or addiction for example, then treatment may be an option *if* it is affordable, available, and/or accesible.[8] Often mental illness leads to criminal behavior before there is a chance for treatment. While some criminal justice agencies offer treatment for mentally ill offenders, there are rarely enough services for everyone who needs them.[9]

The American Juvenile Justice System

Local law enforcement represents the front-line workers in the American criminal justice system, and therefore has the most significant role in raising criminals.[10] The extent to which local law enforcement responds to some children as criminals, superstars, or average Joes for similar types of status offenses and delinquent and criminal behavior impacts the likelihood that the children treated like criminals will become criminals.

Children typically enter the criminal justice pathway through the American juvenile justice system.[3]

The American Faith Community

The American faith community is represented by the 2,000 religious denominations that make up the fabric of our country. The most common types of religious institutions are churches, mosques, and temples. Whether they attend services or not, over 90% of Americans say that they believe in God.[11] Although most religious leaders are male, the American faith community, which is primarily Christian, serves a distinctly female clientele.[12]

Research tells us that involvement in the American faith community has numerous benefits, including increased health and mental health. Yet, the faith community's failure to intervene in matters of family violence among its own membership renders it a breeding ground for juvenile delinquency risk factors.[13] The *Ugly Fact* that few faith community leaders are trained to provide such intervention only exacerbates the problem.

Summing It All Up

The village raises a child and a criminal in much the same way. What differentiates between a person becoming a criminal, a superstar, or an average Joe is the village's response to the person during childhood. Both micro-level and macro-level factors are related to criminal behavior. Micro-level factors include biology, personality, and parental and peer influences. Macro-level factors include the influences of human service systems. Micro-level factors were briefly reviewed here because they are important and the public generally pays more attention to them than macro-level factors. However, the purpose of *It Takes A Village To Raise A Criminal* is to shine the search light on the role of five human service systems in raising criminals: education, child welfare, mental health, criminal justice, and religion.

Ugly Fact #1
Education: Some Children Are Deliberately Left Behind!

The Take-Home Message

1. Early school failure leads to disengagement and dropping out.

2. Dropping out of school is associated with criminal justice involvement.

3. Positive teacher engagement and school-based interventions can save generations of children.

Education Is The Key To The Kingdom

School Is Important

School is the first public place that many children get the opportunity to demonstrate mastery and competence outside of their early family environment. Even small children understand the importance of doing well in school. Many of them refer to kindergarten as "big school", understanding that it is far different from staying at home with mom or dad during the day, being taken care of by a family member while parents work, or going to daycare or preschool. Children understand that there are big things to be accomplished at "big school". That is why early failure in school typically leads to disillusionment, frustration, withdrawal, and negative behavior.

The American Education System

The American education system includes public, private, religious, and any other institutional educational setting. Approximately, 90% of American children attend public schools, so the American education system will refer mainly to public school in this chapter.[1] The primary purpose of the American education system is to equip most children with the minimal basic education required for them to grow into working class adults who meet the needs of the prevailing American industries.[2] During the industrial revolution, the purpose of the American education system was to teach children how to work in factories. In the service age, its purpose was to teach children how to perform various skills required for service-oriented jobs. In the current information age, the purpose has been to teach children how to locate, retain, and communicate information.

Stratification & Labeling Theory

Within the context of capitalism, the working class is stratified, or divided up according to education, achievement, and status – with lower, middle, and upper middle classes.[2] Therefore, it is also the job of the American education system to begin the process of grouping children into the three hierarchies. Labeling Theory says that people become what society labels them, so it is efficient to begin to label the labor force as early as possible.

Labeling is done most obviously through the process of tracking young children into remedial, mainstream, and gifted groups in elementary and intermediate schools. In high school, this tracking is continued by steering the gifted children to college preparatory schools and courses. The mainstream children are steered toward regular courses and perhaps vocational training. And the way is made easy for the remedial children to drop out of high school completely, or perhaps be awarded some certification which is deemed less than a high school diploma.[2]

The children who attend college will typically end up in positions of authority over the mainstream children who graduate from high school. The high school graduates will represent the majority of the labor force.[2] The remedial children, many of whom will drop out of high school, will typically populate the lowest socioeconomic rungs, work low-wage entry level and service positions, and be great candidates for early criminal behavior and involvement with the criminal justice system.

Deliberately Left Behind

The helicopter view of the American education system provides a more reasonable backdrop for considering public policy enacted to address the failure of public schools to adequately educate all children, such as the recently implemented federal No Child Left Behind (NCLB) Act of 2001.[3] On its face, the NCLB legislation seems logical because most people can agree that all children should have access to fair and effective public education. However, if the goal of the American education system is to stratify children into the roles required for a capitalistic nation which incarcerates more of its citizens than any other country in the free world, then some children must be deliberately left behind. This is where the roles of the stratified school groups come into play.

Research consistently underscores how children placed in remedial education groups tend to act out their frustration because of their mainstream school failure, which in turn increases the likelihood that they will continue to be marginalized in the school setting.[4] Experiencing marginalization in the setting where one spends most of one's waking hours intensifies the desire to demonstrate competency in some area. Therefore, children who experience mainstream school failure often resort to petty delinquent behavior in order to demonstrate such mastery, which can quickly evolve into more serious delinquent and criminal behavior with increased skill acquisition and opportunity.

No Child Left Behind Act Of 2001

The Basics

The No Child Left Behind Act of 2001 was passed mainly to try to close the academic achievement gap between white and minority children so that no child would be left behind.[3] The most public concerns of the NCLB Act have been the academic achievement gap between minorities and non-minorities, failing schools located mainly in lower socioeconomic urban areas, astonishingly low high school graduation rates among minority children, and teacher development.

The Historical Context

Taking a step back, it is important to note that the NCLB Act is an amendment of the Elementary and Secondary School Act of 1965, and that it continues the legislation which started state-wide end-of-grade testing in the 1970s.[3] Research indicates that along with end-of-grade testing came the magnification of school failure based on: the achievement gap (and early negative labeling), grade retention, and administrative discharge of children from high school before they graduate. Research suggests that measures of academic progress should be based on such indicators as class grades and promotion through grades levels, in addition to end-of-grade testing.[1] As long as state-defined achievement tests remain the primary measuring stick for academic progress, then certain children will be deliberately left behind in the American education system. Let's take a look at why.

The Achievement Gap

What Is It?

According to the NCLB Act, the achievement gap is defined as differences in scores on standardized achievement tests (e.g., end-of-grade testing, proficiency tests) between minority and white students, as well as advantaged and disadvantaged students. The disadvantaged children are most likely to be African American and Hispanic children who score significantly lower on the tests than the more advantaged children, who tend to be white and Asian.[3] What is interesting is that research shows that both disadvantaged and advantaged African American children tend to score lower on the tests than both disadvantaged and advantaged white students.[5] So, it appears that the distinction between advantaged and disadvantaged applies mainly to those differences noted among white children.

When Does It Show Up?

The official achievement gap first rears its ugly head around the 4th grade, when most children begin taking standardized achievement tests.[1] Often called end-of-grade testing, teachers and administrators usually stress the importance of these tests (especially since the advent of such legislation as the NCLB Act) and most children understand that these tests are a big deal. Children are also aware when they themselves, as well as others, fail to do well on these tests. Even though there can be lots of anxiety when facing these tests for some children and school personnel, along with various rates of preparation for the test, children see themselves as failures when they do not do well on achievement tests. Just a few negative episodes with standardized school testing can increase anxiety so much that children would not be able to do well on the test even if they had designed the test and memorized the answers.

How Is It Calculated?

The achievement gap can be calculated in a variety of ways, depending upon the test used. For example, the National Assessment of Educational Progress (NAEP) is a standardized test that is administered to 4th, 8th, and 12th graders in the United States every year. The achievement gap based on 2005 test scores for 12th graders is represented in the following manner. The percentages of 12th graders who demonstrated an overall understanding of the testing material (basic achievement) in reading were 79% (white), 74% (Asian), 60% (Hispanic), and 54% (African American). The percentages demonstrating at least basic achievement in math were 70% (white), 73% (Asian), 40% (Hispanic), and 30% (African American).[6]

Whose Fault Is It?

On its face, it appears that the responsibility for achievement lies within each child and his family. However, the reality is that school achievement requires equal parts child-related elements (preparation and performance) and school-related elements (teacher expectation and implementation of appropriate school-based interventions). Too often children who fail to achieve at a standard level have limited family-based resources and must rely mainly on school-based interventions if they have any hope of having access to an adequate education.[7]

The most essential elements of child preparation are consistently attending school ready to learn (e.g, being rested and nourished), reading on grade-level, and demonstrating self-control. The performance piece is simply the ability of the child to successfully learn and translate her knowledge to the academic task she faces (e.g., spelling test, written assignments, achievement tests). The extent to which children bring these elements with them into the education system impacts the likelihood that they will achieve at standard levels. Yet, there is still the matter of the school-related elements.

Very little attention is given by the lay public to the significant impact of teacher expectations on school achievement.[8] When teachers are mentioned in the school achievement equation, it is usually related to their own academic and professional achievement and training (e.g., achieving certification of one type or another). Rarely is any attention given to the role of teachers' own biases (both positive and negative) in student achievement, or what contributes to those biases.[9] However, any teacher, student, or parent can identify the teachers' pets and pests in any classroom. The way in which teacher biases are played out in the classroom impacts every child in the classroom, both positively and negatively.

Facing the Achievement Gap: Jo & the Other Joe

Take the case of Jo, a mild-mannered female 4th-grader of lower socioeconomic status who has a history of low school achievement and an uninvolved single parent. If Ms. Smith sees a spark in Jo, perhaps because she reminds Ms. Smith of herself as a young child in the 4th grade, or better yet her daughter when she was that age, then Ms. Smith is going to give Jo a little extra positive attention. She will be able to look past Jo's shabby clothes and the fact that her mother never responds to notes or comes to school meetings or teacher conferences. Ms. Smith will make sure that she always has extra snacks so that Jo can have two on the days when she seems especially hungry. And she will make sure that Jo takes a book home from the library to read every day, providing additional school-based resources to assist Jo.

Jo will try extra hard to please Ms. Smith so she can continue to get the goodies she has to offer, and she likes when Ms. Smith seems proud of her. Jo will get to school a little early or stay a little late to talk to Ms. Smith about the books she reads, and will ask her questions to get a better understanding. In this way Jo's lack of home-based preparation will be overcome by Ms. Smith's positive bias, which includes standard expectations about Jo's academic achievement.

Then there is the other Joe. His story is the same as Jo's, except he is active like most boys his age. However, Ms. Smith sees his shabby clothes, hungry eyes, and his rambunctious behavior and she is reminded of all the stereotypes she has ever heard about kids like Joe. Even though she does not know Joe personally, she will believe all the negative things that other teachers will tell her about Joe and treat him accordingly. Now that her lens is set to a negative bias, then every negative thing about Joe will be magnified. Ms. Smith will be annoyed about the fact that his mother never responds to notes or comes to the school for anything, she will be stingy with the extra snacks, and she will limit Joe's access to school-based resources such as books from the library because he might lose the books.

Joe will not come to school early to talk to Ms. Smith because she will either ignore or reprimand him throughout the day, providing no incentive for spending extra time with her. When Joe begins to act out because he can see that Ms. Smith is treating him differently from the other Jo and the other students, then Ms. Smith will believe that her concerns have been validated.

With the extra attention from Ms. Smith and the school-based resources, Jo feels connected to school and her teacher, she has attended school daily, and she has improved her reading skills. Therefore, Jo will perform at standard levels on the achievement test at the end of the year. In contrast, Joe will fail to perform at standard levels on the achievement test because he feels disconnected from school, victimized by his teacher, and did not have access to school-based resources to help him to improve his reading skills. In addition, he missed as many days of school as he could due to illness, suspension, and truancy because of his lack of connectedness. So, while Jo will be promoted based on her performance, despite her slow start and her lower socioeconomic status, Joe will be lucky to be on the receiving end of a social promotion.

The Ugly Fact of Teacher Bias

The *Ugly Fact* is that, despite well-meaning legislation, some children are deliberately left behind. The truth is that children like those in our example would benefit from the same positive treatment and standard expectations. When a teacher decides not to extend the positive courtesies to any child for any reason, then she is choosing to leave that child behind.[10]

Note that a teacher's positive bias is often related to the ability to relate to the child in some personal way. The more alike the teacher and the child, the more the teacher will be able to identify and engage with the child. In contrast, the less alike the teacher and the child, the less likely the teacher will be able to identify and engage with the child. Add a lack of engagement with the child to negative stereotypes of the group to which the child belongs, along with negative labeling of the specific child, and one has the perfect recipe for school failure for the child who is part of the out-group (e.g., racial or socioeconomic).[9]

Institutionalized Human Behavior

Now if the teacher were asked about her behavior towards either child, it would be easy for her to justify both sets of behaviors applied to similar children. However, she might have some difficulty identifying the positive and negative biases played out with each child, and perhaps the reasons for them. However, this is a perfect example of how institutionalized human behavior (automatic reactions to similarities, differences, and positive and negative stereotypes) perpetuates itself, regardless of the players, and how deliberate decisions are made that result in children being left behind in the American education system.[9]

A Note on the Other Ten Percent

Although 90% of American school children attend public schools, it is important to briefly consider the situation in non-public schools before we leave this topic.[1] While it is true that children attending private, parochial, religious (and other) schools are more likely to have parents who are involved in the school setting and are invested in ensuring that their children are prepared for the learning environment, this is not always true. And while it is true that most children who attend such schools are white and privileged, again, this is not always true. This is why the same dynamics experienced by black, brown, and disadvantaged children in public schools are also experienced by such children in non-public school settings, and for the same reasons. Therefore, the entire American education system is subject to the same institutionalized human behavioral forces involved in creating superstars, average Joes, and criminals.

Graduation Rates

The Legacy of the Achievement Gap

With the achievement gap being what it is, there is no wonder about the disparity in graduation rates between minority and white children. When black and brown children consistently score on achievement tests at rates significantly lower than white children, regardless of their socioeconomic status, there is no reason to expect parity in graduation rates. The impact of consistently failing to achieve according to mainstream standards takes an emotional and social toll on minority children. This toll has its most salient impact when tallying up high school graduation rates.

The NCLB Act Definition

The NCLB Act defines high school graduation rates as the percentage of students who graduate with a regular high school diploma in 4 years.[1] According to 2004 statistics, high school graduation rates were 70% overall, 80% (Asian), 76% (white), 58% (Hispanic), 53% (African American), 49% (Native American), 74% (female), 66% (male), 75% (suburban), 73% (rural), 71% (town), and 60% (urban).[11] One can see the gap between the graduation rates for minorities (except Asians) and the overall graduation rate as well as the rate for white students. In addition, graduation rates for students in urban schools (which have a sizable population of minority students) are far below the rates of schools in non-urban settings. The gap between male and female graduation rates completes the statistical explanation of why African American males in urban schools have the lowest high school graduation rates.

Dropping Out

It should be noted that children drop out of school socially and emotionally well before they do so physically. School failure is a powerful incentive to avoid school. Younger children do it by disengaging and tuning out in the school setting, while older youth do it through truancy or by dropping out of school altogether.[4] It is easy to look into an elementary classroom to see the glazed-over and distracted looks of those children who know that they are not doing well and that nothing is being done to help them. They are just doing time in the classroom. The smarter students among this unfortunate group may act out in order to get some attention (negative or otherwise) and to pass the time.

Grave Implications

The seemingly individual decisions made regarding whether to help students who are struggling with basic skills have grave implications for students. Those students who receive even the most modest school-based intervention in elementary school have a significant chance of being lifted up out of the stream of educational failure.[7,10] In contrast, the decision to withhold such services to struggling children will consistently add up to early school failure, disengagement, truancy, then dropping out (or being forced out through such measures as administrative discharge). The fact that black and brown children are so often in the group that does not receive such services and who ends up dropping out is of particular note.[11]

Failing Schools

The NCLB Act Definition

From a macro-level perspective, failing schools provide the most reliable way to ensure school failure for the largest groups of students. The combination of (1) inadequate resources for school-based interventions, (2) large class sizes, (3) significant numbers of disengaged children, (4) teachers with little insight regarding their student engagement practices, and (5) directives to meet state-based achievement standards despite these conditions yields the right circumstances for a large number of failing children, by which failing schools are defined. The NCLB Act defines failing schools as those whose students fail to make adequate progress towards state-defined achievement standards for two or more years.[3]

Research indicates that labeling a school as failing based solely on achievement test scores is a mistake, regardless of the nature of the achievement tests.[1] Unfortunately, decisions are made based on this labeling process which have enduring and far-reaching effects for both students and schools (e.g., being designated as a failing school, elementary school students not being promoted to the next grade, high school students being denied a high school diploma). Therefore, being labeled a failing school is something to be avoided at all costs.

Fear of Failing

The fear of being designated a failing school leads school administrators to do things that increase the likelihood that struggling students will be positioned for easy entry into the criminal justice system. Dating back to the 1980s, the most controversial trends have been retaining children in the grade prior to the testing grade and pushing them out of high school. These trends have resulted in an overall decrease in national high school graduation rates. Youth who fail to graduate from high school are significantly more likely to become involved in the criminal justice system.[1]

Grade Retention

Retaining children in the grade prior to testing commonly happens in the third grade (preceding 4th grade testing with national assessments) and ninth grade (preceding 10th grade testing with national assessments). This serves the purpose of removing struggling students from the testing pool, but it increases the likelihood that the students will not be retained in school through high school graduation.[1] So, while schools might increase the percentage of students scoring at the proficient level on achievement tests for a particular year, many children's academic careers are negatively and permanently impacted by being deliberately left behind.

Administrative Discharges

Pushing high school students out of school under the guise of administrative discharges is a particularly tricky way to fly below the radar of elevated high school drop-out rates. In some instances, high schools have administrative discharge rates that triple the official drop-out rate.[1] High school students who are discouraged from attending schools which still have time to provide academic assistance have very limited prospects.

Some of them might attend adult education courses to prepare for a general equivalency degree (GED) or to complete their high school diploma requirements.[1] However, the majority of them will end up floating around without either of these credentials and will become stuck in poverty. Therefore, most will live a life of poverty and/or crime, often mirroring intergenerational patterns of school failure, poverty, and criminal behavior, consistent with the stratification necessary for America's capitalistic economy.

Teacher Development

The Context for the Discussion

We consider teacher development last because it has very little to do with children deliberately being left behind. As with failing schools, even poorly trained teachers have much to offer children when they care to give them the best that they have. With achievement depending so heavily on teacher expectations and implementation of school-based resources, one of the most important things about a teacher's skill set is her ability to engage with a child and to help him to gain an appreciation for himself and his ability to learn.[7-10]

While it makes good sense that a properly-trained teacher will be able to provide a higher quality learning environment, it does not necessarily mean that she will have a greater propensity to engage with children who are different from her, especially those who are struggling with their basic skills. Given the opportunity to choose, children fare better with someone who is engaged with them and has their best interest at heart, regardless of their training. Even if the lack of training impedes a higher level of learning, achieving basic skills and maintaining a positive perspective on school increases the chances that the child will remain engaged in the American education system long enough to have other opportunities for advanced learning.

Unqualified or ....

Having set the context for this discussion, let's take a look at the issue of teacher development. The media's focus on unprepared teachers and the movement towards certification for teachers prompted by the NCLB Act easily gives the impression that public school teachers are among the least capable of teaching America's children.[3] In response to the achievement gap issue, accusations are made that somehow teachers are graduating from college with little ability to read, write, and do math themselves, which severely limits their ability to teach those skills to children. Their lack of training is further explained by some saying that teacher pay is so low that it only attracts those college graduates who can not do anything else.

Although post-secondary education is rife with its own issues, most people do graduate from college with advanced skill sets which include enough reading, writing, and mathematics to be able to teach elementary and secondary school children. Further, most teachers today are those who love children and/or those who have spouses whose incomes afford teachers the opportunity to work both regular hours for very little pay and excessive extra hours for no pay. As a result, most teachers are women who accept low wages for the privilege to teach children.[12]

....Disengaged?

The solution to the perception of lack of teacher preparation has been to require teachers to demonstrate their teaching competency by passing certification and licensing tests.[3] This has drawn the ire of many teachers, and well it should, because no attention is paid to the fact that teachers are doing a fine job of teaching white children their basic skills.[6] Therefore, the crucial question is not "Can they teach children to read and write?", it is rather "How do teachers respond differently to black/brown and white?" It is this differential response which almost guarantees school failure for black and brown children who struggle with basic skills.

The Final Analysis

The Stark Reality

The American education system is a primary human service provider, but teachers and administrators rarely see themselves as such. Although aware of the importance of education in general, education professionals minimize the negative impact their everyday decisions have on children at the lowest end of the achievement spectrum. They see the primary responsibility for student achievement as that of the students and their parents.

Like every human being, education professionals respond more favorably to positive situations than to negative situations. This results in teachers being much more responsive to children who are well-prepared for school, have active parental involvement, and are similar to them. Even in the absence of preparedness and parental involvement, as is often the case for low-achieving students, group similarity between the student and the teacher can be enough to prompt the teacher to engage with the child in order to improve the child's academic achievement.

Low School Performance

The decision to refrain from engaging with low-achieving students who are not like the teacher has grave consequences for the children that go beyond the classroom and the school house. Research tells us that over half of all children involved in status and criminal offenses have low school performance.[4] That percentage increases when adult criminals are surveyed.[1] Additionally, low parental involvement in the education system is often correlated with a history of school failure for the parents. So, intergenerational school failure can be traced right back to the school house for previous generations.

Many Hands

Therefore, it is imperative that education professionals appreciate the role they have in raising average Joes, superstars, and criminals alike. Everybody loves to have a hand in raising superstars, their names are always highlighted among the school's accomplished graduates. Teachers even like to hear about what happens to their average Joes. But the common response of teachers when faced with the behavior of the criminals that they participated in raising is the shaking of heads and wagging of tongues. When education professionals understand that those in the greatest need of personal engagement and school-based interventions are those children who are struggling with basic skills and behavior problems, and are without the parental support and the individual attention that every child needs, then more superstars and average Joes will arise out of the group of children who are normally the primary candidates for the criminal justice system.

Saving Generations

Converting even one child from the latter group into the two former groups can save generations of children from the experience of school failure and the associated long-term negative consequences.[4] In fact, research shows that at-risk children can be directed towards positive behavior (such as academic achievement) despite their surroundings when just one caring adult makes a personal connection with them.

Herein lies one of the greatest opportunities for the ultimate goals of teacher development and school enrichment. The ideal situation is for the "daytime parent" to be the person with whom children form a personal connection and who serves as a conduit to all of the school-based resources the children need. Until this becomes a more widespread occurrence for children on the fringe of academic achievement, the American education system will continue to play a primary role in raising criminals.

Summing It All Up

The *Ugly Fact* is that deliberate decisions are made which result in children being left behind in the American education system. The deliberate decision to leave children, who struggle academically, behind by withholding personal engagement with teachers and school-based resources results in early school failure. Grade retention and administrative discharges ease the way to dropping out altogether. Children who are deliberately left behind and pushed out of the American education system are prime candidates for the criminal justice system.

Ugly Fact #2
Child Welfare:
Helping *And* Hurting!

The Take-Home Message

1. The American child welfare system can be as much a hindrance as a help.

2. Welfare reform has added to the ranks of the poor and working poor, leaving mothers and their children vulnerable to criminal behavior.

3. The effects of foster care placement can be more negative than the effects of the environment from which children are removed.

The American Child Welfare System

Safety & Security

Like most human service systems, the American child
welfare system operates at both the state and local
levels, with some national input. The core of the child
welfare system typically consists of state departments of
social service, which include welfare programs and child
protective services. Welfare programs provide cash,
food, and medical assistance to poor mothers, while
child protective services provides for children whose
parents have problems caring for them independently.
In some states these services are provided by the same
state agency, while they are provided by separate state
agencies in others.[1]

Hindrance & Help

The core responsibility of the American child welfare
system is to ensure that children's basic needs are met.
These needs would include safety, shelter, food, and
clothing. It is the one system that is positioned to help
hurting children. Unfortunately, it too often ends up
being as much a hindrance as a help. Perhaps as a
reflection of its hurtful role in needy children's lives,
neither form of child welfare is looked upon favorably.
Being the recipient of cash based welfare assistance has

a stigma, and being the recipient of child protective social services comes with its own set of complexities.[2]

Welfare: The Big Picture

Children whose parents can not provide for them their basic needs and who therefore find themselves in need of child welfare services often fare poorly on a number of levels. If their mothers are dependent upon welfare, they are typically among the poorest Americans. Unlike the public outcry associated with the picture of the 'Welfare Queen' living high on welfare fraud, the reality is that welfare does not provide a living wage for most recipients. In addition, recent welfare reform has resulted in many families trading barely living on welfare for poverty-level wages, often from multiple jobs which can lead to absent parenting.[3]

Foster Care: The Big Picture

Among children who find themselves in the custody of the child welfare system due to insufficient and/or harmful parenting or absent parents, their fate is dubious at best.[2] Foster care is often associated with little emotional or familial attachment and multiple movements. This lifestyle often leads to behavioral problems, homelessness, and criminal justice system involvement.

The Role of Welfare Reform
In Raising Criminals

Putting a Face on Welfare

In 2007, the average monthly welfare caseload for the entire nation was 4 million people (3 million children, and 1 million adults).[4] If we take a look at the type of people who find themselves on welfare, we find mainly single women who have had multiple children by their early 20s.[5] Most of them have little education and few job skills, and are on welfare as a primary means of taking care of their children's basic needs.[3] As stated before, the "Welfare Queen" is not the typical welfare recipient.

It is difficult to miss the fact that most welfare moms did poorly in school, so they have little formal education.[3] *Ugly Fact #1* detailed the role of the American education system in raising criminals through early school failure, grade retention, and administrative discharge of high school students before they receive high school diplomas. In the instance of welfare reliance, we can see how these core mechanisms for deliberately leaving some children behind in the American education system can lead to early and multiple pregnancies, welfare receipt, welfare discharge, working poverty, unemployment without welfare or unemployment benefits, and direct and indirect involvement with criminal activities.

Welfare: Helping and Hurting

While welfare was originally designed to provide a safety net for poor women and children, it brings with it a complex set of undesirable circumstances. Research details the low self-esteem, depression, anxiety, and poor physical health experienced by women on welfare. On the one hand, individuals experiencing these issues are less able to work and support themselves and their children, and therefore are more likely to need welfare. However, research documents that dependence on welfare can lead to these symptoms as well. So relying on welfare can lead to a negative cycle of illness and poverty.[6]

Furthermore, having a parent with little money, limited school success, low self-esteem, and mental and physical illness often results in below-average cognitive stimulation and development, limited resources for educational activities, and uncertainty about nutrition and access to adequate amounts of food for young children. These circumstances make it difficult for children to participate fully in school.[7] Add to these circumstances generations of school failure which reduces the likelihood of mom becoming an involved parent, and the stage is set for an additional generation poised to be deliberately left behind in school, thus creating great candidates for future welfare and criminal justice involvement.

The Details of Welfare Reform

The Personal Responsibility and Work Opportunity Act of 1996 (welfare reform) is the latest attempt to cut spending on welfare by moving poor mothers (and their children) off the welfare rolls and into permanent jobs.[6] The purpose of welfare reform was apparently to empower welfare moms to support themselves independently in order to improve their lifestyles and to save tax payers money. So, welfare was changed by implementing a program called Temporary Assistance to Needy Families (TANF), which offers a five-year lifetime limit on cash assistance, food stamps, health insurance, and programs designed to help welfare moms to learn the skills needed to help them to obtain employment. Research shows that many women have moved off the welfare rolls since welfare reform, but that the success of welfare reform has been dubious at best.[6]

Strain Theory & the American Dream

As a result of welfare reform, the parent-related risk factors for criminal justice involvement have intensified because many welfare moms have been converted from the non-working to the working poor. Strain Theory tells us that people commit crimes when they can not afford the luxuries that they see all around them. Thanks to television and other media, America has painted the picture of itself as the richest nation in the world.

So, when impoverished children and adults see the riches of celebrities and even those next door or several streets over, they believe that they should have a share of those riches.[3] When they realize that they have been shut out of the American Dream because they have neither the money, education, nor the legal means to get the things they want on their own, then they are more likely to figure out how to get the things they want illegally.

Leaving Welfare

Moving women off the welfare rolls has not necessarily meant that they obtained jobs that pay a living wage, nor has it resulted in permanent employment or leaving welfare permanently. The typical mother leaves welfare temporarily for a low-wage job in retail, fast food, child care, and temporary work of all kinds.[3] She maintains some of her food stamp and health insurance benefits while she is out working.

Her self-esteem and mental health improve some.[6] She works until her job or her tolerance for the low wage work runs out. When possible, she works until she is eligible for unemployment insurance when the work runs out. When resources from the most recent job are exhausted, she returns to full-time cash assistance until she is ready to try her hand at employment again. So much for wholesale self-sufficiency.

Unintended Consequences

Research indicates that only about 15% of women who leave welfare do so for full-time employment (e.g., at least 30 hours per week) for a sustained period of time (e.g, two years). Even those who get full-time employment for at least two years contend with low wages. They often find that any 'extra' money they make in comparison to being on welfare goes to child care, medical coverage, and food costs. As a result, these women often continue to feel the financial strain and food insecurity felt by those still on welfare.[6] Perhaps the thinking of the policy makers is that the psychological benefits of working to earn a living might offset the limited economic benefits of working for this small group of welfare leavers.

The realities associated with welfare reform tell of the unintended consequences. Because many moms are leaving welfare for low-wage jobs in retail, fast food, child care, and temporary work of all kinds, they often find themselves juggling long hours or multiple low-wage jobs in an effort to take care of their children.[3] This means that many mothers are less involved in important child care activities such as supervision of physical safety, homework, social involvement, meal preparation and consumption, and peer involvement. Lack of supervision places their low-income children at increased risk for involvement with risky behaviors that are associated with juvenile delinquency.

Up a Creek......

In contrast to the successful welfare leaver who works low-wage jobs for a long time, and those who work temporarily and return to welfare, as many as 30% of mothers who leave welfare find themselves off welfare, but without full-time employment.[6] Although some women in this category leave welfare because they get married or cohabitate with others who can help them financially, many women are discharged from welfare because of rule violations and paperwork errors. Women who have children to care for with no legitimate financial assistance, employment, or welfare are at increased risk for becoming involved directly or indirectly in criminal activities in order to pay their bills and feed their children. These types of circumstances are just the ones that place low-income children at risk for growing into criminals.

....*Without a Paddle!*

If we asked welfare policy makers whether the intent of welfare reform was to create conditions that would more efficiently yield criminals, the answer would have most assuredly been a resounding NO! However, one quick glance at the research on risk factors for criminal involvement for both low-income adults and their children would have revealed that this would be one of the unintended consequences of welfare reform. Yet, given the dependence of the American criminal justice system on America growing its own criminals, one has to wonder whether these unintended consequences are so unintended.

The Role Of Foster Care
In Raising Criminals

Who Is in Foster Care?

There are approximately 500,000 children in the American Foster Care system at any one point in time.[8] The average child in foster care is a 10 year old white male who was neglected by his biological parents and now resides in a foster care family home. About 40% of children in foster care are white, 32% are African American, 19% are Hispanic, and 52% of are boys. In addition, babies less than 1 year old are more likely to enter foster care in any one year than any other age group.

The average time in foster care is 2 years and 4 months, about one in four children (24%) lives with a relative in foster care, while about two in four (46%) live in a foster family home. Most children are released from the foster care system back to their parents (53%) or another relative (11%). Interestingly, about half of the population of children in foster care is discharged from the system, and half come into the system, each year.[8]

How Do They Get There?

Although policies and procedures can differ from state to state and from agency to agency, child protective services are usually initiated by a telephone call to an anonymous hotline to report suspected child abuse or neglect. The more specific information the caller can provide about the child, such as home address, parents' names, and specific details about the circumstances and incidents, the better. Many such calls come from concerned neighbors and loved ones. However, many human service professionals (e.g., teachers, physicians, substance abuse counselors, psychologists) are required by law to report knowledge of suspected child abuse and neglect.[2] Therefore, telephone calls can come from almost anywhere.

One can imagine that the number of telephone calls far outnumbers the resources available to follow-up on the telephone calls. Therefore, the local child protection office has to place the calls in the order of perceived importance, and follow up on those calls in that order. The order of importance can be based on the situation described, the familiarity of the family to the agency, and/or the number of telephone calls received about the same family. Immediate signs of physical danger are often considered ahead of signs of neglect, although neglect is the most common reason that children come into the foster care system.[9]

The first step in following up on a telephone call is the attempt to verify the information received in the telephone report. The parents, the children, teachers, neighbors, and anyone else who might be able to provide information related to the welfare of the children are interviewed in order to obtain a clear understanding about how the children are treated. It is important to note that children are typically interviewed outside the direct presence of another adult (which often happens in school), and that child protection workers do not need parental permission to interview children if their safety is in question. If the telephone report is supported by all the information gathered, and children are indeed thought to be in danger, then the least disruptive option is usually chosen in order to protect the children.[2]

Family preservation intervention strategies such as parenting classes, child protection monitoring, counseling, medical attention, and other needed human services are among the least disruptive options offered to families whose investigations result in significant findings.[2] When these services improve the lives of the affected families and allow children to remain in their families, this represents the child welfare system at its best. However, in order for the services to be effective, the parents must be willing to cooperatively participate in the services....and this is not always the case.

Foster care placement can come after a series of interventions by the local office of social services designed to keep the family together have failed, and it can come suddenly when children are judged to be in grave danger or are completely unsupervised. Parental addiction and incarceration are two primary reasons that children end up in foster care.[2] The case of Jo and her brother Joe, in Jo's own words, paints a picture of a typical route to foster care.

Who Are the Children?
Jo and Her Brother Joe

Hi, I am 4 years old. I mostly live with my mother and brother Joe. He's 6 years old and goes to big school. Lots of times me and Joe live with our grammy too. Sometimes I go to preschool, but mostly I stay home with my mommy and watch TV all day. Mommy has lots of friends and they come and go all the time. Sometimes they bring her stuff, and she tells me to go in the room.

When I get hungry and I come out to find her, she looks funny and says funny things or she's not home. Sometimes I can reach the cereal box on top of the refrigerator and sometimes I can't. When she's not home and the cereal box is empty, I go outside to look for somebody to give me food. I used to be scared, but now I'm used to it. When Joe gets home from school and I'm by myself, he calls our grammy, and we go stay with her.

The last time that happened, grammy got mad and said she was calling "chile proteckshun". Next thing I know, a lady came to talk to mommy one day when she was looking funny, and Joe told me somebody talked to him at school. All of a sudden, I was going to preschool, we had a lot of food, mommy's friends stopped coming over, mommy was going to some classes, and another lady came to see about us a lot at night. But then little by little, all that stuff started not happening. Mommy stopped going to her classes, she stopped taking me to preschool everyday, and her friends started coming over again.

Then one day, the lady came when mommy was looking funny and saw mommy's friends cooking some stuff on the stove. Everybody ran out and left me and mommy there with the lady. The lady called the police, and they came and took my mommy away. The lady went to the room, got some of my stuff, and put me in her car. We went to pick my brother up from school. My brother told the lady to call my grammy. My grammy came to pick us up. We gotta stay with my grammy until mommy gets through with her classes again. I miss mommy, but at least I get to go to preschool and eat and not have to be scared at home by myself.

What Is Foster Care Like?

Foster care placement can take place in the home of a loving relative, and with perfect strangers.[9] Foster care can be temporary or permanent. While in foster care, children may be allowed to see their parents if it is safe and the parents are available and interested. Foster care can result in family re-unification, termination of parental rights, adoption, and/or aging out of the foster care system. However foster care placement is experienced, the interruption of attachment and bonding is the primary route by which foster care results in creating prime candidates for the criminal justice system.

Attachment Theory

Attachment theory says that children bond with caretakers who consistently and predictably meet the children's basic needs for food, emotional connection, and safety.[9] Forming an attachment bond with a primary caregiver is one of the most important ingredients for developing moral character and a healthy sense of oneself in the world. When such bonding does not happen, the child develops a chronic sense of being in danger (of starving, being abandoned or hurt) and perceives himself as having limited value to the world around him. As a result, the child sees herself as worthless and unimportant, and she develops an offensive stance towards her environment which tells her that she is responsible for her own survival, which she needs to ensure by any means necessary.

When attachment is disrupted by multiple foster care placements, this often means that children will have a very difficult time forming secure attachments to any one individual.[9] When children are bounced around from placement to placement like second-hand possessions with no respect shown for their humanity, then it is no wonder that they have problems with attachment and that they learn to get all they can while they can – including attention, food, and anything else they need but can not count on getting from setting to setting.

Adapting to Foster Care – The Upside

Some children are able to internalize the best of their caretakers and take those positive memories with them to each successive placement. The children have usually had a least a small amount of time with someone with whom they formed an attachment bond (e.g., someone who genuinely made them feel loved, valued, and safe). These children learn to adapt to each new environment with more or less success by focusing on previous positive experiences, trying to fit into the current setting, yet remaining emotionally detached from those around them. Such children are intelligent, might have a talent for which they are consistently recognized from setting to setting, and are engaged in the school process. Even small amounts of positive recognition help to grow the children's coping ability, which becomes part of their resiliency.[9]

While this stance may be adopted under the chronically uncertain conditions of foster care placement, when such a child encounters predictability and consistency over the long term, she will do everything she can to test the truth of the placement. He will act out in all of his old ways, and even come up with some new adventures. The *Ugly Fact* is that most people do not understand that foster children can be expected to do worse behaviorally in a long-term stable setting before they do better because of the trauma of their past experiences.[10]

The unexpected paradox of the foster child finally getting the stability that all children need is that somebody has to "do time" for all the instability of the past. Very often those new to the child welfare system are not prepared for the acting out and emotional trauma that can be expected proportionate to the child's total experience of instability – both within and outside of the child welfare system - prior to coming into more stabilized care. This is often the reason for frequent movements and disrupted adoption placements for even the most resilient child.[10]

Adapting to Foster Care – The Downside

The children who do not manage to form an attachment bond with someone in order to get the message that they are loved and valued tend to act out their anger and disappointment while in foster care placement. Their acting out tends to guarantee that they will be moved from placement to placement, which feeds the cycle of disruptions that interfere with attachment, that results in multiple moves.[9] In the unlikely event that such children have the opportunity for long term foster care placement or adoption, their acting-out will also intensify before it gets better. Ancillary services, such as respite care, are important to support long term caregivers of behaviorally disruptive children.[2]

Disruption in attachment and lack of bonding can lead to all sorts of mental health problems for children. The most common are PTSD, night terrors, bed-wetting, depression, separation anxiety, conduct disorder, oppositional defiant disorder, addiction.[9,11] Bonding with a caretaker is the primary way that children learn to experience emotions towards themselves and others.

When the primary caretaker is emotionally positive and loving towards the child, the child feels the caretaker's positive emotions and learns to feel those emotions for the caretaker. These are essential ingredients for developing empathy and morality. In contrast, the lack of bonding with a caretaker makes it very difficult for children to experience genuine positive emotion towards themselves and others. This has a negative effect on self-esteem and makes it difficult to form lasting emotional bonds with others.

Foster Care – The Aftermath

To be sure, most former foster children go on to live productive lives. Yet, children who spend time in foster care have more developmental problems than other high risk children. For example, they are more likely to have school (poor achievement and grade retention), mental health (depression, anxiety, post-traumatic stress disorder), social skills (poor peer relationships), and behavioral problems (aggression, difficulty with impulse control) than other low income children.[9] Most of these problems can be traced to disrupted attachment caused by experiencing parental maltreatment and having multiple caregivers during childhood.

The increased difficulties which result from having a history of foster care placement often endure into adulthood. Former foster care children often face a life of homelessness, addiction, and criminal justice involvement. An estimated, 30% of homeless people have a history of foster care placement, with as many as 20% of people in shelters coming directly from foster care placement. Further, as many as 80% of some samples of criminals have histories of foster care placement.[11]

The Final Analysis

The Ideal

In its most ideal form, the American child welfare system provides a safety net for children whose parents are unable to care for them in one form or another. Providing temporary financial and medical assistance to poor mothers who need such help to maintain a stable home for their children is the least intrusive way to help needy families. In the best of all situations, poor mothers would be able to maintain stable employment which paid a living wage and use welfare only in dire emergencies.

The Ugly Fact

The *Ugly Fact* is that the role of the unintended negative consequences of welfare reform in raising criminals needs to be considered. The fact that many mothers leaving welfare are rendered either working poor or without legal income at all places both them and their children in jeopardy of direct and indirect involvement with criminal activity. This is one of the most efficient ways to raise criminals.

Good Intentions

If the intention of welfare reform is to move women from welfare into jobs that will help to sustain a reasonable lifestyle, then we know from years of research that there are a number of effective employment transition models that can be followed. For example, research on supported employment programs for individuals with mental illness (which would describe many of the women who have problems moving from welfare to work) details the combination of continued financial assistance, mental health services, and on-the-job training that participants need in order to improve their job skills and their mental health enough to sustain employment.[12]

Some would argue about the ongoing cost of such programming. However, such programs could be paid for with existing job-readiness training dollars being spent on programs that do not work.[12] The return on investment of supported employment programs which would elevate women from poverty-level wages and/or criminal involvement to support their children would be priceless.

Disrupted Attachments

Like welfare, foster care is designed to provide temporary assistance to children whose parent can not care for them either temporarily or at all. Foster parents, whether loved ones or strangers to the child, open their homes and often their hearts to children during a time of great need. By definition, children come into foster care due to adverse parenting experiences, which makes them more sensitive to the challenges they will face in foster care placement.[9]

Although the foster care system varies from place to place, it is reasonable to expect that foster care placement resources in most places are limited, especially areas where the demand is high. In addition, because of policies, resources, foster care parent training, characteristics of the children, human capacity, and length of time in foster care, multiple placements can be expected. However, it is the disruption in attachment that occurs because of multiple placements which is thought to be a key cause of the short-term and long-term challenges faced by children in foster care.

The Sun Will Come Out Tomorrow

Although there have been improvement in foster care practices and policies as a result of research and related policy changes, it is imperative that parents, care givers, and administrators understand that children who experience foster care need more support than even the typical at-risk child. Careful attention needs to be paid to the challenges created by parental maltreatment, disrupted attachment, multiple caregivers, and the myriad of co-occurring circumstances (such as school failure and behavior problems) which beset the typical foster child in the form of appropriate and accessible services during and after foster care placement.[9]

In addition, children who age out of foster care need support specific to preparing them and then transitioning them to live on their own. Although the foster care system is meant to provide short-term services, the reality is that a significant number of children remain in foster care placement for a year or longer and many remain until they age out at 18 years old. Therefore, the children would benefit from long-range planning in addition to having the short-term goals.[9]

Summing It All Up

The child welfare system provides vital services to the neediest children. However, because of institutionalized human behavior, the *Ugly Fact* is that the system hurts as much as it helps. Children whose mother receives assistance with basic needs are stigmatized and have few resources. Children who experience foster care placement as part of child protective services intervention often suffer as a result of disrupted attachments to both their biological parents and their foster care providers.

The child welfare system could benefit from many existing research-based models for assisting welfare mothers with obtaining employment which pays a living wage, as well as for addressing the special issues associated with foster care placement. The solution is a matter of directing resources towards the programs and services that work, instead of relying upon the long-standing experiences and practices that have always driven the child welfare system – rendering the system efficient in the process of raising criminals.

Ugly Fact #3
Mental Health:
Mental Illness Can Be Criminal!

The Take-Home Message

1. The American Mental Health System is made up of public and private mental health professionals who provide services designed to help people function better.

2. Depression, anxiety, and addiction can be viewed as the "common colds" of mental illness. Addiction, PTSD, conduct disorder, and ADHD are commonly found among criminal justice populations.

3. Mental illness can be criminal when it goes untreated and people end up in prison.

Mental Illness

What Is Mental Illness?

Mental Illness is defined as experiencing the symptoms associated with any of the mental disorders found in the Diagnostic and Statistical Manual of Mental Disorders (DSM), which is the most common mental illness classification system used in America.[1] The most common mental illnesses are depression, anxiety, addiction, post-traumatic stress disorder (PTSD), conduct disorder, and attention deficit hyperactivity disorder (ADHD). Depression, anxiety, and addiction can be viewed as the "common colds" of mental illness. Addiction, PTSD, conduct disorder, and ADHD are commonly found among criminal justice populations.

Depression

Depression affects about 10% adults in any year. That translates to about 13% of women, 5% of men[2], and 9% of children (13% girls and 5% of boys).[3] The main symptoms of depression are sadness (or anger and irritability), and problems with eating, sleeping, energy level, and/or thinking for two or more weeks.[1] Depression is more common among females than males, and the difference begins in the teen years. Interestingly, depression tends to look different in males compared with females. Females are more likely to be sad and tearful, while males are more likely to be irritable and angry.

Anxiety

Anxiety affects about 18% of adults[4] and 13% of children[5], with women experiencing higher rates than men in any year. There are different types of anxiety disorders, with one common theme: fear of something. People will go to great lengths to avoid the thing they fear: objects and living creatures, social situations, wide open spaces, and separation from loved ones are just a few categories.

Addiction

Addiction affects about 10% of Americans 12 years or older in any year, with greater rates for males (12%) than females (6%).[6] As many as 50% of juvenile justice populations experience addiction[17]. There are three defining characteristics of addiction (or substance dependence). The first is using alcohol and drugs to the point that they interfere with one's ability to work or do well in school, take care of normal responsibilities (e.g., chores, children), function well in relationships, and engage in hobbies and other normal activities. The second is developing tolerance to the substances such that it takes more and more to achieve the same high. Similarly, the third defining characteristic is withdrawal

– experiencing physical illness and psychological distress when the substances are no longer present in the body.[1]

Post-traumatic Stress Disorder (PTSD)

Post-traumatic Stress Disorder (PTSD) is an anxiety disorder that is worth talking about separately because it is often experienced at high rates by those in the criminal justice system. PTSD affects as many as 50% of children in juvenile justice samples[7], and about 3.5% of adults in the general population in any one year.[4] The hallmark of PTSD is experiencing recurring anxiety as a result of very scary and hurtful experiences.

The recurring anxiety usually occurs in the face of or fear of recurring intrusive thoughts about the past event – often called flashbacks.[1] Although PTSD was mainly associated with military experiences when it was first identified, it is now understood that it occurs among people who experience traumatic assault right in their own living environments. For example victims of all forms of physical and sexual violence are at great risk of developing PTSD.

Conduct Disorder

Conduct Disorder affects 1-4% of adolescents in the general population in any one year, with more boys than girls receiving the diagnosis.[8] Conduct Disorder is a mental illness of childhood, which is a requirement to be diagnosed with Antisocial Personality Disorder later in adulthood. As can be expected, this disorder is also very prevalent among juvenile justice populations (35% to 52%).[7] The hallmark of conduct disorder is consistently behaving in a manner which violates established rules and social expectations.[1] Common rule violations include home, school, curfew, property, and living beings (people and animals).

Attention Deficit Hyperactivity Disorder

Attention Deficit Hyperactivity Disorder (ADHD) affects 5% of Americans children and adolescents[5] and 4% of adults[4] in the general population in any year. Males are four times more likely than females to receive the diagnosis. ADHD is commonly found among juvenile justice populations (35% to 52%).[7] ADHD is the kissing cousin of conduct disorder. The main symptoms of this disorder are difficulty thinking things through, impulsiveness, and extremely limited self-control.[1]

This disorder is related to conduct disorder because many children with ADHD consistently engage in rule violation as a result of their difficulties with self-control.[1] Although it is commonly diagnosed in childhood, ADHD sometimes endures into adulthood, and can be first diagnosed in adulthood as long as the same symptoms were present in childhood. Most adults diagnosed with ADHD in adulthood can vividly recall experiencing the symptoms as children, whether they were diagnosed or not.

The American Mental Health System

What Is It?

The American mental health system can be hard to figure out and navigate. The core of the American mental health system is a network of mental health professionals who work for private companies (including themselves) and public agencies (e.g., publicly-funded agencies which are paid to provide services mainly to the poor and uninsured). There can be great differences in who receives treatment in the public and private sectors of the American mental health system.[9]

Private Providers

Private providers typically operate out of leased and owned office space and accept private (e.g., Blue Cross/Blue Shield) and public health insurance (e.g., Medicaid) for the mental health services they provide.[9] Private providers also allow people to pay for services themselves and may also offer some free services.

Private providers must be well-versed in the workings of managed care in order to receive payment from insurance companies and Medicaid for their services.

Public Providers

Public providers typically operate out of local agencies which receive both state and federal funding to provide mental health services to those who have Medicaid, do not have health insurance, or who can not afford to pay for such services themselves. Public mental health services are also offered by mental health treatment facilities associated with community and academic hospitals that accommodate all types of paying and non-paying clients. Then there are school-based services that are designed for early intervention with children, as well as those services which are associated with child welfare and the courts (e.g., counseling for foster care children, mental health courts).[9] The most recognizable form of the public mental health system is usually the state-run mental health hospitals where only the severely and chronically mentally ill usually end up for any significant period of time.

Who Does It Help?

In its most ideal form, the American mental health system is designed to help all people address their mental health needs in order to help them function better. There have been many scientific advances in the field that allow trained mental health professionals to help people more efficiently than in the past. However, the stigma associated with mental illnesses of all kinds tends to keep people away from the services that could be of great help to them.[9]

There is even stigma regarding types of mental illnesses. For example, because addiction is often viewed and treated separately from other mental illnesses, it is common for addicts with additional mental illness to say that they will go to drug treatment, but that they will not get treated for the other mental illness. "I don't mind admitting that I'm an addict, but I ain't crazy!" Additionally, research shows that some people are more likely to tell their primary care doctor about their emotional problems than to seek out a trained mental health professional.[9]

Mental Health Professionals

The meaning of the term "mental health professional" can be confusing for the average person. What are the meanings of the many different titles and specialties among mental health professionals? In order to answer that question, let's take a step back and review the basics. There are basically four types of professionals who are widely recognized as mental health professionals: psychiatrists, psychologists, social workers, and licensed counselors.[10] Having a clear definition of each can help the discussion.

Psychiatrists

Psychiatrists are medical doctors who can prescribe medicine and who have also been trained in personality, human behavior, and psychotherapy. Psychiatrists are more likely to prescribe medicine for mental problems than to do therapy. They have national and state licenses to practice medicine and psychiatry.[10]

Psychologists

Psychologists' training includes the Ph.D. in psychology (usually clinical or counseling), by which they receive the most advanced training in personality, human behavior, psychotherapy, and psychological testing (including intelligence, diagnostic, and human development). They are therefore able to provide mental health services from the most common to the most serious mental health problems – but most do not prescribe medicine. They have state-level licenses to practice psychology.[10]

Social Workers

Social workers have a Master's Degree in social work (MSW) and a state-level license to provide psychotherapy. They also provide linkages to other human service resources in the community as needed by their clients. They do not prescribe medication and they do not conduct psychological testing.[10]

Licensed Counselors

Licensed counselors can have a Master's degree in any number of social science disciplines (e.g., agency counseling, psychology,) and have a state-level license to practice counseling.[10] Unlike the other types of mental health professionals whose professional identity is derived from their common education, licensed counselors' professional identity is derived from their licensure. Note that all four types of the most widely recognized mental health professionals must maintain current licenses to practice.

Other Mental Health Professionals

In addition to the four widely-recognized types of mental health professional, there are other less-well-known professionals, who receive varying amounts of training, education, and licensure to practice as mental health professionals. A selection of the other disciplines include marriage and family counselors (education, training, and licensing similar to licensed counselors), substance abuse counselors (practice requirements often ranging from no education or training requirement save for experience as a recovering addict at the entry level – all the way up to Master's Degree in a social science and state-level licensure), psychiatric nurse practitioners (master's degree, licensure, and medication prescription privileges), and pastoral counselors (master's degree in theological training with a concentration in counseling).[9] In addition, there are a whole host of paraprofessionals who provide non-clinical supportive mental health services in all types of settings (e.g., schools, community-based agencies, churches).

Seeking Help

This brief review shows that it can be hard to figure out where and from whom to seek help even if one can cope with the stigma of mental illness. A good place to begin is with a known trusted professional (like a family physician or human service professional) who can usually suggest a professional or an agency to contact for starters.[9] In addition, state and national associations are good places to begin the search for mental health services. The public mental health system is usually much more easily recognizable than some of the private and ancillary settings, and can therefore be a great place to obtain information about mental health services.

Definition of Mental Health Treatment

Now that we have reviewed the different types of mental health professionals, let's briefly review a snapshot of mental health treatment. Medication management and psychotherapy are the hallmarks of mental health treatment.[9]

Medication Management

Medication management involves taking psychotropic medication designed to help those suffering from all forms of depression, anxiety, addiction, and psychosis feel better.[9] Remember that each of these categories of mental illness can cover many specific disorders. Clients must meet regularly with the prescribing physician in order to determine whether the medication is working for the particular person as designed. As with any medication, it is important that psychotropic medication is taken only by the person for whom it is prescribed, in the doses dictated by the prescription.

Psychotherapy

Psychotherapy involves a mental health professional and one or more clients meeting in a private place (and sometimes on the telephone and on the internet) and talking about the problems associated with the clients' mental illness in enough detail to determine the causes of the problems and how the problems should be addressed.[9] Psychotherapy typically occurs in the following formats: one-on-one individual therapy (e.g., cognitive-behavioral therapy, play therapy), multiple-client group therapy (e.g., social skills building, grief support), and drug treatment (primarily group therapy, drug testing, and self-help support groups).

The Role Of Untreated Mental Illness In Raising Criminals

Falling between the Cracks

Both the stigma about mental illness and confusion about mental health treatment easily result in many people who need services falling between the cracks and remaining untreated.[9] Add to the stigma and confusion about mental health treatment the barriers that make it difficult to access services, such as the strict rules of managed care and Medicaid, difficulty paying even small fees for services, long waiting times for services, lack of transportation to obtain services, and a scarcity of specialty services in many geographic areas, and the cracks get wider and wider. Indeed, falling between the cracks can be fatal for those whose mental illness is disguised by poor attitudes and consistently negative behavior. These individuals are often labeled as bad and not worthy of treatment, so they are often the least likely to receive mental health treatment.

Mental Illness Can Be Criminal

Because successive programs of mental health reform dictate that mental illness should be treated primarily in local communities instead of state mental health hospitals, jails and prisons are housing more and more mentally ill inmates. Because of the holes in the American mental health system, the state and federal criminal justice system is usually the safety net for mentally ill persons who fail to receive the mental health treatment they need in their communities. Mental illness can be criminal when a person is put into prison for doing things that result from their (often untreated) mental illness. While most penal institutions have some form of mental health service no matter their sizes, jails and prisons are not equipped to provide mental health services to all the inmates who need it.[11]

Addiction is a mental illness which often results in incarceration for both men and women. For example, research shows that as many as 70% of state prisoners have a history of alcohol or drug addiction.[12] The most recent "War on Drugs", beginning in the 1980s, resulted in tremendous increases in the criminalization of mental illness, especially among African Americans, mainly because of federal minimum mandatory sentences for crack cocaine possession.[13] The great disparity in the penalties for crack and powder cocaine resulted in federal and state prisons being filled with a disproportionate number of African American men, women, and children.[11]

Because addiction is a mental illness that usually begins in childhood and occurs with another one (e.g., depression, PTSD, ADHD), there is often an opportunity to treat at least one of the mental illnesses before either one has a chance to result in criminal convictions. School-based services provide a primary point of intervention for these issues.[9] For example, a child who experiences divorce, abandonment, foster care, or some other form of disruption in attachment is at risk for developing depression. A child who experiences physical or sexual abuse, who witnesses domestic violence, or who lives in high crime neighborhoods is at risk for developing PTSD. The child whose parents had attention and behavioral problems is at risk for ADHD and conduct disorder. Any of these experiences offer an opportunity for intervention and resolution before negative behavior or addiction has a chance to set in. Likewise, any of these issues left untreated can easily lead to acting out, addiction, and criminal justice involvement.

Putting a Face on Untreated Mental Illness Joe & His Girlfriend Jo

Let's take a look at how untreated mental illness leads to prison for Joe and his girlfriend Jo. Joe and Jo met in middle school, where they became fast friends because of their ability to relate to each other's equally dysfunctional family environments. Joe's father physically abused him and his mother. This left Joe feeling angry and helpless.

Before his father began hitting him too, he would often dream of rescuing his mother from his father's drunken rages. When he was about 10 years old, he put one of his plans into action, and his father retaliated with a round of blows to Joe's face and chest that left Joe hurting and winded. Thereafter, when Joe's dad got drunk, he started in on Joe first, and then beat his wife for trying to rescue Joe. This turn of events led Joe to search for a balm for his troubles. In his search, he found marijuana, alcohol, and Jo.

Jo could easily relate to Joe's plight. Jo's father abused her mother, and left her older brother feeling angry and helpless about his mother too. However, instead of fighting his father, Jo's brother let his anger out by physically and sexually abusing his even more helpless little sister Jo. This went on for 2 years until Jo told her maternal grandmother about it.

When Jo's grandmother confronted her mother with the information, Jo's mother refused to believe it. Besides, she did not want to raise such an issue with her husband. So, grandma made an anonymous call to child welfare. Investigation substantiated the allegations, and the plan called for separating the children from each other, as well as from their father. Jo's mother refused to separate from her husband, so Jo and her brother ended up in foster care. Jo went to a foster care home, while her brother went to an institutional setting.

Jo was feeling terribly depressed and traumatized from her experiences when she met Joe, and she and Joe clicked right away. Joe introduced Jo to marijuana and alcohol, and they used the two to soothe their pain all through middle and most of high school. Neither one of them received any counseling for their emotional pain. So, around 9th grade, Joe needed more of a high to distract him from his ongoing physical abuse, and decided to try a little cocaine to see how it worked. He started with powder, and then moved on to crack. He liked both of them, but alcohol was more of his thing. But he did see crack as a way to make some money.

In making his decision about joining the drug trade, he introduced Jo to crack, to see what she thought about it. He thought she would like it, but that she would prefer alcohol or marijuana like he did. Surprise! Crack was just what the doctor ordered for Jo. She encouraged Joe to start selling crack in the summer after their 9th grade year.

With a steady supply of crack from Joe, Jo quickly became addicted to crack. She spent a lot of time with Joe and understood all about the drug trade at the entry level. Joe took care of Jo's addiction and she watched his back all through high school. They each managed to graduate from the high school remedial program, mostly because of Jo's insistence that they at least go to class each day. But they knew there was no college in sight.

Therefore, Joe moved up in the drug trade and Jo's addiction intensified. Joe kept Jo near and supplied her with crack. But that all changed when Joe got shot in the leg in a crack deal gone bad. He spent many weeks recuperating and Jo eventually smoked her way through all of Joe's remaining crack stash and his money. Feeling bad about being out of commission for weeks and for not being able to take care of Jo, Joe started taking more of his pain killers than he needed to ease his physical pain and was soon addicted to his pain medication, in addition to the alcohol and the marijuana. Jo began to take over some of Joe's duties in the drug trade to earn money to live on and to get crack.

When Joe got back on his feet, he decided to get revenge on the person who shot him, a fellow low-level drug dealer. Joe shot his rival, and stole his drugs and his money. Based on a tip, the police located Joe and found the drugs and the money and the weapon on him. He and Jo were arrested on the spot. A legal search of their apartment revealed Joe's drugs and money. They were both looking at long-term crack time.

Preventing Untreated Mental Illness From Leading To Prison

In light of the stigma, confusion, and access barriers associated with mental health treatment, the mental health system could be proactive in addressing mental illness at three important intervention points: primary, secondary, and tertiary prevention.[9] Since research clearly defines the challenges associated with mental illness, the conditions that give rise to mental illness, and the negative consequences associated with untreated mental illness, one has to wonder whether the consequences are so unintended when individuals in the mental health system decide to leave some individuals untreated.

Primary Prevention

As with most things relating to prevention, the ideal point of intervention regarding mental illness escalating to criminal behavior is before criminal behavior starts – called primary prevention.[9] The ideal scenario would be for the mental health system to educate children and parents about mental health, including practices and behaviors that promote good mental health (such as protecting children from violence and abuse, and providing adequate parental supervision at all age levels), and those that do not (such exposing children to violence, and disbelieving reports of child abuse). Because children spend most of their waking hours in school, school-based mental health professionals are in a prime position to recognize children who need support through difficult transitions (such as divorce, death, and foster care placement) so that their needs do not escalate to more formalized therapeutic intervention.[9]

Secondary Prevention

The second point of intervention – secondary prevention - is to detect and address known problems so that they will not escalate into enduring problems.[9] In the case of children like Joe and Jo, school-based mental health professionals are in a prime position to detect signs of physical and sexual abuse and addiction, and to know when children are living in transitional situations like foster care so that they can offer assistance and support.[9] There is a great deal of research which highlights the relationship between problem behavior and negative home experiences. When school-based mental health professionals ignore signs of mental distress and instead support an emphasis on harsh disciplinary practices over sound mental health strategies, they take the first step towards criminalizing mental illness.

Tertiary Prevention

Tertiary prevention – the third point of intervention – involves managing mental illness so that it does not continue to result in revolving criminal justice involvement.[9] Addiction is one mental illness which typically results in repeatedly going in and out of prison. Research indicates that treatment works best for addiction when it occurs for at least 6 -12 months and is accompanied by aftercare and involvement in self-help groups.[14]

Unfortunately, most people with addiction do not receive this level of treatment in their communities. While there is drug treatment in prison settings, there is not nearly enough to treat everyone who needs it.[11] Moreover, it is not the mission of most penal institutions to treat mental illness. Therefore, the lack of access to sufficient community-based mental health treatment will mean continued criminal justice involvement for many.

Tossed to the Winds

When the mental health system is shrouded in barriers to access, managed care policy restrictions, lack of insurance coverage, and inadequate treatment duration and capacity[9], then those whose mental illness remains under-treated and untreated are tossed to the criminal justice winds by default. Mentally ill mothers who drive their children into rivers, drown their children in their own bathtubs, and throw their children off bridges while everyone shakes their heads in knowing disbelief are criminals created in the same fashion as African-American crack addicts caught up in the "War on Drugs" and mentally ill college students who shoot students in lecture halls and on campus quads. There is prevention for the mental illness that ails America, but it is dependent on the behavior of individuals within the American mental health system.[9]

Treating Mental Illness
In Criminal Justice Settings

Mental Health Courts

Looking for a way to treat mentally ill criminals instead of sending them to prison, the federal government developed the mental health treatment courts (e.g., drug courts) model. This treatment model tends to serve non-violent offenders whose crimes are related to their mental illness. When they meet certain requirements, addicted convicted criminals, for example, can be offered the option of attending treatment and complying with a treatment plan, while remaining both drug and crime free, instead of incarceration. They are required to come to court for a progress report, which usually includes a formal report by the counselor and a drug test. If any of the rules are broken, they can be incarcerated right away. Mental health courts appear to be one way to facilitate access to mental health treatment for mentally ill criminals.[14]

Prison-Based Drug Treatment

Because so many people in prison have histories of addiction, federal legislation implemented drug treatment in federal prisons, and provides grant funding for drug treatment in state prisons.[11] To a great extent, the federal prison system has been among the first to implement research-based drug treatment practices, and then to evaluate the success of treatment in these programs. The state of the art of drug treatment in the federal prison system is long-term residential treatment, lasting for about 9 months. The greatest result of treatment comes when treatment is delivered at the end of the prison sentence and the person becomes involved in treatment aftercare and secures a job when he leaves prison.[15] Research shows that for every $1.00

spent on drug abuse treatment, there is a $7.00 return on the investment. In contrast, the money spent on incarceration alone usually yields a 50% re-incarceration rate.[11, 14]

The federal government also supports drug treatment in state prison systems through special programs encouraging long-term residential treatment similar to what is offered in the federal prison system. However, sentences tend to be much shorter and institution requirements and conditions tend to be much different in state prisons, so it can be difficult to replicate in state prisons drug treatment offered in federal prisons.[11]

The Final Analysis

The Ugly Fact

The American mental health system is designed to treat people with mental illness efficiently and humanely. However, due to stigma and confusion regarding mental health treatment, managed care, limited private and public health insurance coverage, and other barriers to treatment, many more people are affected by mental illness than the American mental health system treats. Failure to provide treatment for most people who suffer from mental illness is not benign neglect. Instead, the *Ugly Fact* is that some people's untreated mental illness (e.g., ADHD and addiction) results in a steady progression of negative behavior, which leads them to criminal behavior, conviction, and incarceration. This is so true that the criminal justice system is said to be the safety net under failing public mental health systems. However, the criminal justice system does not function as an effective mental health system.

Prevention Is Important

At each possible point of intervention in the prevention process (primary, secondary, and tertiary prevention), real people make the decision to intervene or not. Each decision to intervene or not has important consequences for both the person with the mental illness and the larger community. For example, the decision not to help children who experience painful loses and family circumstances equates to the decision to set them on the mental illness road to the criminal justice system.

By Any Means Necessary

Those who participate in people falling through the cracks in the mental health arena must keep in mind that mentally ill people and their illnesses are not going to go away just because they are ignored. The child who does not receive support and guidance while going through a negative transition such as divorce or death of a parent will emerge as the adolescent who is acting out in class and with parents. The untreated adolescent becomes the angry young man who begins his revolving criminal justice career as a 16-year-old who feels he must survive "by any means necessary". Be on the lookout for the mentally ill, criminally-skilled man he becomes in neighborhoods across America, sooner or later.

Summing It All Up

Depression, anxiety, and addiction are among the most common mental illnesses in the general population. Certain types of mental illness (e.g., addiction) are much more common among criminal justice populations than the general public. The *Ugly Fact* is that the criminal justice system is often the "safety net" for those who go under-treated or untreated in either the private or public American mental health system. The criminal justice system does provide mental illness management in most cases, but it is not designed to provide comprehensive mental health treatment for all who need it.

The human beings responsible for designing and implementing mental health policies would do well to take note of mental illness among criminal justice populations in order to determine a more efficient way to address mental illness before people progress to criminal behavior. We know for a fact that it is cheaper to treat mental illness than it is to incarcerate people. For example, research shows that for every $1.00 spent on drug abuse treatment, there is a $7.00 return on the investment. In contrast, the money spent on incarceration usually yields a 50% re-incarceration rate. Most would agree that the 700% return on investment from treatment is good business for everyone!

Ugly Fact #4
Juvenile Justice:
Finishing School for Criminals!

The Take-Home Message

1. The American Juvenile Justice System began with a mission of rehabilitating youthful offenders.

2. The media's exaggeration of the problem of juvenile crime has resulted in more punitive juvenile justice strategies.

3. Developmental prevention strategies are more effective in preventing juvenile crime than punitive strategies.

The American Criminal Justice System

What Is It?

The American criminal justice system is made up of local law enforcement (police officers, courts, and jails), state-level law enforcement (state-level policing agents, courts, and departments of juvenile justice and adult correction, which include probation and parole), and federal law enforcement (federal policing agents, courts, and the Federal Bureau of Prisons – which includes probation).[1] Local law enforcement agents are typically the front-line workers in the American criminal justice system, and therefore have a primary role in raising criminals. The extent to which local law enforcement agents use their discretion in responding to some children as though they were criminals, superstars, or average Joes for similar types of status offenses and delinquent and criminal behavior impacts the likelihood that the children treated like criminals will become criminals through their involvement with the American criminal justice system.

The Historical Account

Local law enforcement officers serve as the front line in detecting and acting on rule violations. People become candidates for involvement in the criminal justice system primarily because their crimes are reported to or detected by police officers.[1] Therefore, local police officers play an important role in the American criminal justice system and in raising criminals.

In the 18th century, the policing role was left mainly to volunteer "watchmen" in urban areas, and constables in rural areas. The local police professionals as we know them today started in New York in 1845 for the purpose of controlling poor minorities (mainly Irish and Native American) who were waging great battles with both the industrial company owners and between themselves. The main goal of the paid professional police force was to keep the peace and to keep the working class and poor from attacking members of the upper classes.[2]

Before long, the professional police model developed in New York and enhanced in other major cities, with the emphasis on professional conduct and keeping the working class and poor in line, spread throughout the country. The model was the foundation upon which state and federal law enforcement agencies were developed. The development of the professional police model led to the development of professional court proceedings and imprisonment.[2]

In fact, the 14th Amendment (1868) called for due process in the decision to deprive people of liberty, life, or property and thus created the mandate for a more professional criminal justice system. Within this more professional system, arrest for rule violation is the first step in the provision of due process. However, it is important to note that resources are limited for processing people for arrest. Therefore, police officers are expected to make judgment calls about whom to arrest and for what.[1] Minor offenses, as are most juvenile offenses (e.g., property offenses), public drunkenness, gambling, and vagrancy provide the greatest latitude for professional discretion.[3]

Purpose of Incarceration

Many people erroneously believe that one important purpose of incarceration is to teach criminals skills that will help them to avoid further incarceration – often called rehabilitation. The *Ugly Fact* is that the purpose of incarceration is mainly to remove criminals from public life as punishment for their unlawful behavior – by keeping them locked away with other criminals.[4] While there is some rehabilitation programming available in most state and federal prison institutions (e.g., education, mental health treatment, employment skills training, and religious services), the reality is that the most common response to incarceration is re-arrest and re-incarceration. So, the best way to prevent continued criminal justice involvement is to prevent initial criminal justice involvement.[5]

Focus on Juvenile Justice

The American criminal justice system includes the juvenile justice system for those younger than 17 years, and the criminal justice system for adults. While it is true that children under 17 years old are often imprisoned in adult criminal justice settings, we will focus mainly on the Juvenile Justice System for the purposes of this discussion.[1] Many criminals in adult prisons start their criminal careers in the Juvenile Justice System.

The American Juvenile Justice System

The Historical Account

Prior to the professionalization of law enforcement and the criminal justice system, property offenses, public drunkenness, gambling, and vagrancy formed the cornerstone of punishable behavior, with children and adult often punished in the same manner. However, there were some who believed that children and adults should be treated differently for breaking society's rules. The beginnings of the Juvenile Justice System can be traced back to New York (1825) and Chicago (1899) which were the places of the first youth detention center and juvenile justice court, respectively.[4] The leaders of the early juvenile justice movement were called child savers because they operated under the premise that delinquent children should be treated differently from adult criminals. Specifically, it was believed that delinquent children could be saved from a life of crime through nurturing and rehabilitative services.

By 1925, all states followed the juvenile justice model and established special courts and detention centers for juvenile delinquents.[4] The court acted in the place of the children's parents, and consequences included services designed to nurture and teach children the skills needed to live productive lives while they lived in residential settings designed especially for juveniles. Many juvenile delinquents were poor and unsupervised, so there was a focus on providing basic needs and moral education, with no guarantees of "due process" since juvenile custody by the state was considered civil and not criminal. The Juvenile Justice System hummed along this course until the Juvenile Justice and Delinquency Prevention Act of 1974 was passed, guaranteeing juveniles the right to due process given to adults, while still maintaining a focus on rehabilitation.[4]

Current Views: Impact of the Media

At about the same time that the Juvenile Justice and Delinquency Prevention Act of 1974 was passed, the news media began to experiment with news content that would grab the attention of the public most consistently. One focus of these bolder headlines that consistently grabbed public attention was that of crime, and juvenile crime in particular. The media helped to fuel the fear of wildly increasing violent behavior by juveniles that has not been supported by actual data over the past 40 years, but that remains popular today.[5] This public perception of increased violent crime among juveniles drove the focus of the juvenile justice system to an increasingly punitive stance, especially regarding expanding crimes for which juveniles could be convicted and punished as adults.

Current research fails to support the focus on increased punishment for juvenile delinquents. In fact, the research shows that juveniles who are convicted and punished as adults go on to commit more crimes at a greater rate than juveniles who were housed in the Juvenile Justice System for the same crimes.[4,5]

The Role Of The Juvenile Justice System In Raising Criminals

Reasons for Juvenile Crime

Some academic theories say that the reason for juvenile crime is because of the juveniles themselves (e.g., rational choice theory). Others would say that certain structural characteristics of the environment breed juvenile delinquents (e.g., strain theory). The most logical answer is that juvenile delinquency arises from a combination of both types of factors. For our purposes, we will examine the structural factors related to the role of the juvenile justice system in raising criminals.

In examining the juvenile justice system, a number of facts should be noted. While the juvenile justice system may be less culpable in raising criminals than the criminal justice system, it still plays a major role in raising criminals. The juvenile justice system has an over-representation of African-American, and to a lesser extent, Hispanic youth. Additionally, most juvenile delinquents (about 64%; roughly 2 out of 3) commit a small number of crimes for which they are identified and convicted. In contrast, only about 15% (roughly 1 out of 7) are considered chronic juvenile offenders who are responsible for at least 75% of all juvenile crimes committed.[5] It is these chronic offenders who have the greatest likelihood of growing into adult criminals.

Typical Practices

Today's juvenile justice system is based more on the philosophy of deterrence than (re)habilitation as it was in the past. The notion of deterrence is based on the idea that planned interference with criminal behavior and sure and swift punishment of a certain magnitude will stop individuals from committing crime in the first place, or committing crime again. However, research indicates that the main strategies of deterrence increase criminal recidivism (returning to prison), instead of decreasing it. Punishment and confinement are two main strategies of today's juvenile justice system which increase recidivism.[5]

While rehabilitation (teaching new skills to prevent recidivism) is the preferred method of responding to juvenile delinquents, not all rehabilitative efforts are effective with them. Research indicates that many popular rehabilitation efforts do not effectively reduce recidivism among juvenile delinquents. Group behavioral treatment (e.g., social skills and criminal thinking interventions) and substance abuse interventions are among the most popular, yet largely ineffective, rehabilitative methods offered to juvenile delinquents. [5]

Punishment

Research indicates that the very premise of a punitive juvenile justice system constitutes the failing parts of the system. Specifically, research indicates that punishment does not deter juvenile delinquents from their criminal behavior. In fact, some studies show that the threat of punishment for delinquent crimes actually increases juvenile delinquent behavior.[5] This suggests that there is something positive associated with being punished that reinforces criminal behavior.

Confinement

Confinement (1) in large juvenile reformatories and (2) adult prisons (3) for long periods of time almost guarantees that juvenile delinquents will continue to commit crimes. Any of these three conditions of confinement alone leads to increased recidivism because of an increase in offender management concerns and a decrease in treatment services.[5] In addition, the increased interaction with other criminals under these three conditions allows for the validation of criminal identity and culture, wherein confinement is viewed as a right of passage or respite from the streets.

Group Behavioral Treatment

Research shows that juveniles involved in group treatment settings serve to reinforce the criminal identity and culture. Groups that are formed for such interventions as anger management, social skills training, and peer intervention have the side effect of creating negative relationships that can increase criminal behavior.[5] Juvenile delinquents have skills to teach one another, but they are not typically positive in nature.

Substance Abuse Interventions

In the main, there is no overwhelming evidence that, drug testing, drug courts, and typical substance abuse treatment programs reduce recidivism among juvenile delinquents. The challenge of the effectiveness of these approaches appears to be two-fold: the notion of the ineffectiveness of deterrence strategies (drug testing and drug courts) and the absence of family, school, and community involvement in the interventions (all three interventions).[5]

Profile Of Juvenile Delinquency

Reason to be Concerned

The review of the American criminal justice system and the role of the juvenile justice system in raising criminals can be quite discouraging. To consider that not every adolescent is arrested for every status offense and crime that they commit, and that current methods of punishing those who are arrested and eventually confined to juvenile and adult criminal justice settings do not work is indeed discouraging. In fact, these issues underscore the reason why most people would rather ignore the problem of juvenile delinquency – especially when they believe that it does not exist in their communities.

However, it will not do to remain either discouraged or unconcerned because all of society is responsible for children who do not receive effective services to stop their juvenile delinquency before it leads to adult criminal behavior. Recent headlines highlight how unchecked juvenile delinquency can show up even in the most privileged environments and cause widespread grief.

Who Killed Eve Carson?

Let's consider the progression from juvenile delinquency to adult criminal behavior of the young men who have been arrested and charged with killing Eve Carson, University of North Carolina at Chapel Hill's 2007-2008 student body president on March 5, 2008: Demario James Atwater (age 21 years) and Laurence Lovette (age 17 years).[6] Atwater's documented march toward criminal behavior began with his dropping out of high school in 2002 (at age 15 years). Laurence Lovette spent 14 months confined in the juvenile justice system before dropping out of high school in 2007.[6,7]

Demario James Atwater

The official record of Atwater's criminal behavior indicated that he managed to stay out of trouble for 3 years after dropping out of high school. Atwater's record of previous convictions included breaking and entering a home in 2005 (at age 18 years). He received 3 years probation and was required to pay the victims $1,900. He was convicted of violating his probation for the previous conviction because of having a handgun in June 2007. However, the revocation of his probation was delayed until November 2007, due to reported failed supervision by the probation officer assigned to his case.[6]

We can see that Atwater was helped along his criminal career by the education and criminal justice systems. Had he at least been engaged in school long enough to obtain a high school diploma, he might have been in school and/or gainfully employed in 2005 instead of breaking into someone's house to steal less than $2,000 worth of merchandise. Additionally, had he been in prison instead of on 3 years of probation within a broken system, he would not have had a handgun in 2007. Had his probation been revoked as required by law for having the handgun in June 2007 or even November 2007, perhaps he would not have been available to be accused of participating in Eve Carson's killing on March 5, 2008.

Laurence Lovette

Lovette was in jail for breaking into someone's house in November 2007, the same year he dropped out of high school.[6,7] He was given $20,000 bail, and stayed in jail until January 16, 2008, when he was given a 24-month suspended sentence. Two days later, on January 18, 2008, Duke University graduate student Abhijit Mahato was found dead in his apartment. On February 2, 2008, Lovette was arrested again for having a stolen vehicle in his possession. He was given $2,500 bail and released. He was arrested again on February 4, 2008 for burglary, given $10,000 bail, and released the same day.[7] Eve Carson was killed on March 5, 2008. By March 13, 2008, Lovette was charged in the murder of both Mahato and Carson.

A friend of the family noted that Lovette was adopted and that he started his negative behavior after his adoptive father died.[6] It would appear that Lovette was supported in his walk towards adult criminality by at least four of the systems that should have helped him: child welfare, education, mental health, and juvenile justice.

Unless he was immediately adopted as an infant from a short-term temporary foster care placement, it is very likely that Lovette experienced multiple home placements while in the custody of the child welfare system, which would have resulted in interruptions in bonding and increased sensitivity to future separations. Had the mental health system been available to him when his adopted father died to help him to process his grief over yet another parental separation, he might have had the opportunity to channel his youthful energies elsewhere.

Had the education system embraced him and engaged him, he would have been attending high school instead of being in and out of jail and available to participate in the killing of two college students in the space of four months. Finally, had the juvenile justice system offered proper rehabilitation programming, he might have made maximum use of his 14-month confinement and learned skills needed to make better choices once his confinement ended.

Juvenile Justice Strategies That Work

Prevention Is Important

The profile of juvenile delinquency highlights the need to focus on programming that works to keep youth from engaging in status offenses and criminal behavior, and will turn juveniles away from these behaviors once committed. As we can see, the problem of juvenile delinquency belongs to entire communities, and will not go away just because it is commanded out of someone's else's backyard. As the Carson and Mahato killings indicate, problems that we do not address systematically right in our backyards will be sent away to grow, and then show up as unchecked monsters on the doorsteps of even the most privileged among us. Investing in strategies that work to help our children avoid or minimize involvement in juvenile delinquency makes good sense for everyone!

The good news is, and there is always good news, that there are strategies that work to help children who have the profiles of those who grow up to be criminals. The best practice is to concentrate significant effort and resources toward early prevention with young children with behavior problems, early intervention with child delinquents 6-12 years old, graduated sanctions for juvenile delinquents 13-18 years old, and developmentally-appropriate mental health treatment for everyone along the continuum.[5]

Research indicates that about one out of three young children with disruptive behavioral problems will go on to engage in some form of juvenile delinquency as children. Further about one out of three child delinquents will go on to be chronic delinquents and adult criminals. It is these two groups - those with disruptive behavior problems as young children and those who are at highest risk for going on to become chronic delinquents – who should receive the most intensive juvenile justice system interventions.[5]

Juvenile Justice Intervention Model: Comprehensive Strategies

Comprehensive Strategies is a comprehensive Juvenile Justice System intervention model being implemented in some urban areas which includes services that reduce the chances of later delinquency by addressing needs across multiple domains. In the main, Comprehensive Strategies involves the interdependent cooperation between juvenile justice and the other child-serving systems that typically operate separately and typically use the juvenile justice system as the safety net for the children who manage to fall between their many cracks: education, child welfare (including cash assistance and foster care programs), and mental health.[5] By channeling resources to the highest risk children and coordinating services to tighten up existing gaps within and between systems, there is evidence that significant numbers of children can be diverted from their trajectory towards a lifetime of criminality.

Children who have early contact with child-serving agencies because of their own or their parents' behavior (e.g., disruptive behavior at school, neglectful or abusive parental behavior) have been identified as a primary target group. Additionally, poor children, and those who live in crime-ridden neighborhoods have been identified as prime candidates for comprehensive juvenile delinquency prevention strategies.[5] Such strategies provide the most benefit when they meet the developmental needs of the target population.

Prevention Strategies: Birth to Age 5 Years

Family management improvement programs (or parental coaching) are highlighted as a first step in the delinquency prevention continuum from pregnancy to six-years old. These prevention services are most effective when implemented during infancy and early childhood, prior to referral to social services for child abuse or neglect. Teaching parents of babies, toddlers, and young children parenting strategies regarding age-appropriate supervision, nurturing and guidance, and discipline are important first steps in the primary prevention of juvenile delinquency.[5] Parenting strategies targeted towards the prevention of physical and sexual abuse at this age are especially important for preventing juvenile delinquency among girls.[5]

For example, a study of parental coaching provided via a visiting nurse program serving poor unmarried pregnant mothers and poor teen mothers through the second birthday of their babies proved to be an effective delinquency prevention program up to 15 years later. Also, research has shown that parent training (via home visitation) and early childhood education for the parents of two- to six-year-olds reduced juvenile delinquency among high risk populations assessed up to 20 years later.[5]

Prevention Strategies:
Ages 6 - 12 Years

The importance of incorporating education-based prevention services starts at age two. So, it is not surprising that school-based interventions are the hallmark of prevention for youth ages 6-12 years. The primary goals of school-based strategies are teaching behavior control skills to improve positive behavior and promoting school engagement to improve academic achievement and investment in the school setting. For example, teacher-led behavior management games which reward children for taking control of their positive behavior, along with clear and consistently enforced school rules related to pro-social behavior in school settings have been shown to reduce disruptive behavior associated with later delinquency for this age group.[5]

Prevention Strategies:
Ages 13 - 17 Years

For youth ages 13-17 years, the prevention efforts tend to straddle school and community, consistent with the developmental challenges for this age group. So, the hallmarks of prevention services include mentoring by an adult and community-based gang prevention programming (to include the prevention of associating with gangs even if one is not a member), violence prevention classes at school, and family crisis intervention services for children facing distressing family environments.[5] Clearly, this age group requires the most cooperation by child-serving agencies in order to provide the array of juvenile delinquency prevention programming needed.

Early Intervention With Child Delinquents: Ages 10 years and Under

Research shows that children who become delinquents at 10 years or earlier come from home environments ripe for raising criminals: domestic violence, child abuse, addiction, adult criminal behavior, and mental illness. Some research indicates that the authority of juvenile court is needed to enforce participation of parents in the coordinated services of cooperating child-serving agencies: education engagement, behavioral and social skills training, parenting education, and mental health services. The intensity of intervention services needed to intervene successfully with this group and their families can be viewed as "parenting" the entire family. Research indicates that such coordinated service delivery can result in a 60% reduction in further criminal behavior for first-time juvenile offenders.[5]

Graduated Sanctions

A system of appropriate, planned, and consistent negative consequences is needed for youth whose delinquent behavior is not prevented or decreased by prevention or early intervention strategies. The hallmark of an effective system employs graduated sanctions, with levels of increasingly restrictive punishments (up to confinement in a juvenile justice facility) for subsequent infractions. Graduated sanctions may begin with the least restrictive level (e.g., intensive probation supervision) and move up to the most restrictive level (e.g., confinement), or it may begin with most restrictive level and move down to the least restrictive level.[5]

The levels below confinement usually include a menu of community-based treatment services which mirror those provided during early intervention. The difference is that there is increased juvenile justice oversight of juveniles' involvement in the programming. Research indicates that graduated sanctions combined with treatment services (both community- and institution-based) can reduce recidivism for as many as one in three chronic juvenile delinquents.[5]

A Note About Girls

Prevention and intervention strategies must include measures that are responsive to the impact of sexual and physical abuse on juvenile delinquency for girls. Girls are especially at risk for sexual and physical abuse throughout childhood and adolescence.[5]

The Final Analysis

Finishing School for Criminals

In the final analysis, the American Juvenile Justice System plays an important role in the raising of criminals. As is typically rendered, this system serves as finishing school for youth who begin their walk towards criminality with difficulty in school and failure to have their needs appropriately addressed by the child welfare and mental health systems. By the time a child reaches the juvenile justice system, there is often no turning back from a lifetime of criminal behavior for about 1 out of 3 of them. Although most juveniles initially become involved with the juvenile justice system as a result of non-violent property crimes, about 1 out of three continues to re-offend, which can escalate to much more serious adult crimes.

The Ugly Fact

The *Ugly Fact* is that typical violence prevention and juvenile justice system strategies are not working to decrease juvenile delinquency or criminal recidivism despite the assumptions upon which public opinion and public policy are based – that increased punishment will prevent or stop juvenile delinquency. Instead, research shows that the solution to the problem is to be found in the historical roots of the child savers movement - developmentally-appropriate delinquency intervention strategies. These strategies make sense for everyone, because there is no getting around the fact that preventing and stemming juvenile delinquency is the responsibility of entire communities who face the consequences of chronic juvenile delinquency.

Summing It All Up

The *Ugly Fact* is that typical juvenile justice system strategies of punishment for the purpose of deterrence utilizing confinement for long periods, in large juvenile facilities, and in adult criminal justice facilities do not prevent delinquent behavior – and in fact sometimes increases delinquent behavior. Instead, research shows that the most economical answer to the question of what will work appears to be the coordinated efforts of the child-serving agencies to treat the multiple psychosocial problems that ail children and their families before they have the chance to begin acting out their angst. Prevention programming needs to be effective for only one or two youth in order to save the lives of people like University of North Carolina at Chapel Hill's 2007 - 2008 student body President Eve Carson.

Ugly Fact #5
Faith Community:
Breeding Ground for
Juvenile Delinquency!

The Take-Home Message

1. The American faith community serves mainly women and yields many benefits.

2. The church's failure to respond to abuse renders it a breeding ground for juvenile delinquency.

3. Needed: Prison Prevention Ministries.

The American Faith Community

What Is It?

The American faith community is represented by the 2,000 religious denominations that make up the fabric of our country. The most common types of religious institutions are churches, mosques, and temples. Whether they attend services or not, over 90% of Americans say that they believe in God.[1]

Among other things, the purpose of organized religion is to offer a structured opportunity for believers to meet together with fellow believers around their common religious beliefs. These beliefs typically center on an all-powerful God who meets all human needs and the command that humans help less-fortunate others – rendering many religious organizations de facto human service agencies funded primarily by the local congregations.[2] Research tells us that there are many benefits to be derived from participation in a faith community, including increased physical, mental, and emotional health, and increased pro-social behaviors. As with therapy, more women participate in the faith community than men.[3]

Religion & Juvenile Delinquency Prevention

Adults are not the only members of the faith community to benefit from participation. Research indicates that regular participation in a faith community is related to decreased involvement in juvenile delinquency in general, and especially among African American males who live in high-crime urban neighborhoods.[1] In particular, youth who attend church services regularly are thought to be insulated from the criminal behavior around them because of the positive structured activities, supportive social network of adults, and increased engagement with school and positive peer groups. Additionally, African American male youth residing in poor, chaotic environments can escape the ills of these environments through regular involvement with church activities.

While these results certainly provide empirical support for generations of anecdotal observation, the fact that religious institutions are primarily patriarchal in leadership and have a majority female client base can not be ignored.[3] So, some would say that it is no wonder that males who append themselves to a primarily female environment on a long-term basis manage to stay away from criminal behavior. The argument could be made that they are not the kind of boys who would engage in criminal behavior or associate with deviant peers anyway. Further, it is easy to see how the number of males who participate regularly in the faith community dwindles with age, with a bit of a resurgence in participation among males who marry. Therefore, the real question is if the faith community has so much to offer, why does it fail to consistently engage older males?

The Role Of The American Faith Community In Raising Criminals

Ills of Society

The American faith community has always served as a defacto human service delivery system because the ills of society are also found among members of the faith community. Although most central religious figures are male, the American faith community, which is primarily Christian, serves a distinctly female clientele. Because religious doctrine often dictates that men are the leaders of women, it is of no surprise that the male leaders of the faith community rarely speak out or intervene on such human service matters as male-perpetrated domestic violence, child physical abuse, or child sexual abuse.[4,5] This is true despite the fact that in recent years the American government has formalized the faith community's position in the human service delivery system by providing funding for the faith community to provide any number of human services interventions.[1]

Deadly Silence

In light of its role as an important community-based
service provider, the faith community's glaring lack of
response to social ills such as abuse within its own
membership creates a breeding ground for juvenile
delinquency risk factors. Family factors are primary
sources of risk for juvenile delinquency. Domestic
violence and child physical and sexual abuse are among
the top three family factors that place children at risk
for juvenile delinquency.[6] The faith community's silence
on these matters perpetuates generations of family
dysfunction and risk for criminal involvement.[7]

The Faith Community & Domestic Violence

Domestic violence can be defined as intimate partner
violence which is used by one partner to control the
other one – usually the male controlling the female.
Broadly, domestic violence can take the form of
physical, emotional, mental, financial, and even religious
control. Women have a 28% chance of experiencing
domestic violence in their lifetime.[7] The fact of women's
second class positioning in most religions has rendered
the notion of such issues as male perpetrated violence
against women a complex issue for the church to
consider. Most religious doctrine place women and
children in a submissive position in relationship to men,

and violence is often seen as a necessary part of ensuring such submissiveness.[4,5]

Even when faith community leaders do not support violence, it is very difficult for them to confront men about their behavior. Leaders of the faith community often view domestic violence as a private family matter between a man and his wife, and few are qualified to address domestic violence.[5] When women do seek assistance regarding their suffering from the faith community, they rarely find compassion or guidance that places their safety first. They are more likely to encounter advice that supports the notion that men have a right to achieve submission from their wives by any means necessary. Rarely are women counseled to leave a domestic violence situation. And still rarely are men called out about their abusive behavior.[8]

Wife vs. Mule

This situation is problematic on a number of levels. If we just take the perspective of valuing a woman as much as a mule, it is a poor farmer who cripples his mule and expects him to still be able to plow a field. Such is the man who physically wounds and mentally cripples his wife and still expects her to manage his household and raise his children. Men often take little thought of the negative consequences that result from domestic violence. Domestic violence has consequences which reach far beyond the moment and a man's need to control his wife.

Consequences of Domestic Violence

One of the main consequences of domestic violence is the wholesale fear and helplessness that is engendered in all the members of the household.[7] The wife is terrified wondering when her husband will strike the next time. She spends a good deal of time trying to make sure that she does what she needs to do to avoid being abused, and is therefore not able to give the children the emotional nurturing they need for their own proper development.

This means that mom might be less able to give infants and toddlers what they need to learn self-control, younger children might not get the cognitive stimulation they need to be prepared for kindergarten, and older children might not receive the attention to their behavior or school work needed to ensure their success. Ultimately, dad's violence toward mom teaches children that violence and lack of self-control is ok. These consequences place children at direct risk for juvenile delinquency.[6]

Child Witnesses Are Harmed

People often think that children are not directly harmed by domestic violence as long as they are not the target of abuse. However, children witness most domestic violence events, and they are traumatized by it just as if they had been abused themselves.[7] The children are filled with fear and rage about their father, even if they are not the targets of the father. Children often go back and forth between wanting to protect their mother from their father, and hating her for allowing herself to be abused. They often lose respect for their mother, and her ability to parent them is further compromised.

Research shows that the negative effects of domestic violence only begin with the trauma caused to the wife and children. For the children, it is a lifelong legacy. It is common for children who witness domestic violence to be very angry, act out violently with siblings and peers, suffer from anxiety and depression, do poorly in school, and have limited social skills. As child witnesses of domestic violence grow up, they are more likely to bring battering into both their dating relationships and their marriages – thus continuing the cycle.[7] Many juvenile delinquents report domestic violence in their families.[6]

Breeding Ground

Given the *Ugly Fact* that domestic violence is a great risk factor for juvenile delinquency, participation in the faith community has been shown to insulate children from criminal behavior, and that women are the predominant members of the faith community, the church is in a prime position to do significant justice by taking a stance to consistently speak out against domestic violence.[5] Yet, by consistently attempting to avoid the topic altogether, consistently refusing to confront perpetrators, and counseling women to tolerate domestic violence in their marriages, the faith community perpetuates itself as a breeding ground for juvenile delinquency.

The Faith Community & Child Physical Abuse

Child physical abuse is another issue that the faith community tends to remain silent about. Child physical abuse comes in many forms, including hitting, burning, scalding, starving, freezing, and any other assault to a child's person. According to the National Child Abuse and Neglect Data System, official records show that about 145,000 children (out of about 74 million children or less than 1%) experience physical abuse each year.[9]

In contrast, surveys of adults in the general population indicate that about 23% of males and 20% of females report experiencing childhood events that were defined as childhood physical abuse by the researchers.[10] Child abuse is mainly perpetrated by biological parents, with mothers more likely than fathers to abuse children.[9] Parents abuse children for a number of reasons, including feeling overwhelmed with parenting, being targets of abuse themselves, and needing to control children.

As with domestic violence and women, notions of children as third class citizens who should be controlled by their parents render this a topic that many faith community leaders do not want to address. Like domestic violence, child physical abuse is seen as a private family matter. Because of religious doctrine, many parents and faith community leaders may not view child physical abuse for what it is, choosing to see it as a legitimate means of discipline for their children.[11]

Trauma of Abuse

Like domestic violence, physical child abuse traumatizes children and renders them angry and fearful. Abused children often fail to develop the positive self-esteem needed for success in so many areas of life. Further, child physical abuse tends to lead to depression, anxiety, post-traumatic stress disorder, children acting out their anger and frustration with peers and in school, and substance abuse and addiction.[10, 12]

Like domestic violence, child physical abuse is the gift that keeps on giving: abused children are much more likely to abuse their own children. And the cycle continues. Children who are raised to believe they are not valued through such experiences as child abuse have little ability to value others. Many juvenile delinquents report a history of child physical abuse.[6]

Prime Position

The faith community is in a prime position to intervene on known and suspected cases of child abuse among its membership in order to stem the tide of a lifetime of negative consequences, including juvenile delinquency. Few parents start out trying to determine the best way to harm their children's bodies and spirits in their perpetration of child abuse. Understanding that children who are treated with the wholesale disrespect that is communicated by child abuse have little chance of growing up to be healthy productive citizens may help faith community leadership to appreciate the benefits of confronting child physical abuse in their communities.[13]

The Faith Community & Child Sexual Abuse

Child sexual abuse is a very sensitive topic, which has been given a great deal of attention in the media in the last decade or so. Child sexual abuse involves the perpetration of a sexual act on a child by someone who is at least 5 years older than the child. This means that child sexual abuse can be committed by both children and adults. According to the National Child Abuse and Neglect Data System, official records show that about 80,000 children (out of about 74 million children or less than 1%) experience sexual child abuse each year.[9] In contrast, surveys of adults in the general population indicate that about 14% of males and 32% of females report experiencing childhood events that were defined as childhood sexual abuse by the researchers.[10] A history of child sexual abuse is reported by many juvenile delinquents, especially girls.

Child sexual abuse is perpetrated against boys and girls mainly by men who are known and loved by the children and their families. This includes fathers, step-fathers, brothers, uncles, cousins, friends of the family, and trusted members of the faith community. While they are all considered sex offenders, they are not always pedophiles. Some people offend against children because they prefer them sexually, while others offend against them because they are available to be used as sexual objects. The sexual violation typically occurs as a result of the relationship and/or close proximity between the child and the perpetrator.[14]

While Catholic priests have received a great deal of attention for the sexual abuse they have perpetrated against children for decades [15], the fact of the matter is that child sexual abuse is more likely to occur closer to home. Some might think that the vow of celibacy taken by priests predisposes them to act out sexually against children, but they are not alone among faith community leadership who sexually abuse children. The *Ugly Fact* is that children may be at risk for child sexual abuse among trusted men in any setting, faith community or not.[14]

The Perpetual Gift

Like domestic violence and physical sexual abuse, child sexual abuse comes with many consequences for the child during childhood. They include trauma, anger, rage, fear, behavioral acting out, sexual acting out, substance abuse and dependence, and impaired social relationships.[14] Child sexual abuse is also the gift that keeps on giving. It is not uncommon for child sexual abuse victims to victimize other children while they are yet children themselves. In addition, while fondling age-mates against their will may be seen more as inappropriate physical contact and not as "sexual abuse", these behaviors are more likely perpetrated by children who have been sexually abused.[16]

As with domestic violence and child physical abuse, the faith community is in the perfect position to intervene in issues related to child sexual abuse in order to stem what is often an intergenerational tide of negative consequences for children and their families and communities. Yet, the faith community leadership typically steps right in line with ignoring child sexual abuse as adamantly as it ignores domestic violence and child physical abuse occurring among its members.[13]

Needed: Prison Prevention Ministry

Two-Pronged Approach

We know from this *Ugly Fact* that, despite its obvious drawbacks, involvement in the faith community has numerous benefits, including juvenile delinquency prevention. Similarly, we know from U*gly Fact #4* that, despite the faith community's recent focus on prisoner rehabilitation efforts, the most efficient way to prevent continued criminal justice involvement is to prevent initial criminal justice involvement.[6] Therefore, it would appear that the most efficient use of the human and financial resources of the faith community would be the prevention of initial criminal justice involvement. This would involve a two-pronged approach: (1) intervening upon the juvenile delinquency risk factors present in the families already involved in the faith community and (2) attracting and keeping children and families with known risk factors involved in the faith community over the long term.

When speaking of prevention, it is always good to have a target and an understanding of the target's needs and the available resources. Research tells us that family problems and school problems are among the major risk factors for juvenile delinquency. Research also tells us that effective intervention across all known risk factors includes having a positive long-term connection with at least one caring adult, involvement in structured positive activities, and interaction with positive peers.[6]

Functioning Families

So, the first thing that faith community leadership can do is to ensure that its members' families are functioning in a manner that is consistent with raising well-adjusted members of their particular faith.[13] While that may differ according to the particular doctrine and culture of each faith, the community can easily assess how well it is doing by evaluating how well families are doing according to common standards. For example, women are very likely to include their children (both boys and girls) in their participation in the faith community when the children are younger.[17] Therefore, keeping abreast of children's school engagement and performance is one way to measure the functioning of the entire family. Children whose families are significantly dysfunctional do not tend to do well in school, thus placing them in jeopardy of juvenile delinquency.

Attracting Men

Knowing that most children who are at-risk for juvenile delinquency are males, we can see an obvious disconnect between their needs and the largely female focus of the typical faith community. So, the question is how can the faith community attract and retain the regular participation of males over 12 years old? The obvious answer is by offering programs that meet the needs of male youth and adults. Designing and carrying out programming for males is likely best done by men, which would necessarily involve their presence and commitment.[18]

Younger and older males tend to like similar activities: those that involve movement and competition. Therefore, programming for them would not be based around sitting in a pew listening to testimonies and sermons.[18] Instead, faith communities that offer baseball, basketball, golf, and other competitive activities for male youth and adults stand a good chance of attracting male participants, coaches, and spectators.

Meaningful Connections

In addition, activities such as facilities maintenance and restoration provide an opportunity for youth to learn trade skills and for men to use their skills to benefit their faith community. Such activities allow the opportunity for fellowship as well as the practice and communication of the faith's doctrine. This scenario also increases the likelihood of youthful males engaging in anti-delinquency behaviors: developing and maintaining meaningful connections with positive male role models, participation in positive structured activities, and interaction with positive peers.

Without the presence of men to attract other males, then perhaps programming can be concentrated on the younger boys who are accustomed to women leading most of their faith activities.[3,17] In this way, the faith community could mirror other human service prevention efforts which are primarily implemented by women. This would allow the faith community to grow its own male leadership who would eventually carry out male-specific programming.

The Final Analysis

First and Last Hope

The American faith community has a very clear role in advancing its benefits to include comprehensive juvenile delinquency prevention programming. The church has many of its own issues, including the failure to adequately address domestic violence, and physical and sexual abuse of children among its members and leaders. These three issues often occur simultaneously, and in any combination. For example, it is not uncommon for a man to beat his wife and sexually abuse his daughter, and/or physically abuse his son. The wife is too afraid for herself to protect her children, and the children are too afraid and ashamed to tell anybody outside the family. Therefore, faith communities often serve as the first and last hope for many women and children whose lives are plagued by the ills that breed juvenile delinquency and adult criminal behavior.

Stepping on Toes

To be sure, courage and innovation are required for faith communities to abandon the role they play in raising criminals. Confronting other adults about what has been traditionally considered private family business is not for the faint of heart. In fact, faith community leadership must necessarily dare to step on toes and pull down masks in the interest of stamping out abusive behavior among their congregants. While this may serve to initially cause concern and perhaps shrink membership rolls, it may eventually lead to a very healthy membership, which will attract those who know they can get their needs met in such communities.

Summing It All Up

The *Ugly Fact* is that the American faith community offers both risks and rewards. One of its main risks is the leadership's lack of intervention in circumstances that breed juvenile delinquency and adult criminal behavior (e.g., family violence). Despite its risks, involvement in the faith community improves any number of lifestyle measures, including health, mental health, and problem behavior. The faith community is poised to advance these advantages beyond the primarily female clientele it now serves, to include comprehensive delinquency prevention programming.

Summary

The Final Take-Home Message

1. The *5 Ugly Facts* are chilling.

2. It takes a village to raise a criminal, average Joe, and a superstar.

3. Effective "community parenting" can guide all parties to responsible adulthood instead of the criminal justice system.

The Final Take-Home Message

Chilling Information

The research presented herein regarding the role that the five human service systems play in raising criminals is chilling at best. To think that the criminal justice system has grown for three decades while high school graduate rates have declined over the same period, and nothing has worked to stem the tide is very troubling. When considering solutions to monumental problems, it is often small behaviors that create the greatest change. In order to slow down and even reverse the progression of the criminal justice system pipeline, the need to make the village a safe haven for all children and their parents is tantamount.

It Takes a Village....

Inherent in the portion of the African proverb that reads "It takes a village to raise a child" is the practice of the community providing direct intervention with children as well as supporting parents as they shoulder primary responsibility for guiding children through childhood into responsible adulthood. Supporting parents amounts to more than providing for children's basic needs along with facts about child development and child management strategies. It also involves attending to parents' developmental needs, which do not disappear just because they become parents. In fact, often times, becoming a parent intensifies adults unmet developmental needs.

Community Parenting

The *Ugly Fact* is that some parents need more support than others in raising their children into responsible adulthood. They require the unified resources of the five human service systems – education, child welfare, mental health, juvenile justice, and religion. When children fail to receive the parenting they need because their parents fail to receive the support they need, the entire community suffers. Therefore we would do well to consider the idea of "community parenting", which would consist of the network of child-serving systems and community agencies actively "parenting" both children and adults alike in order to guide all parties into responsible adulthood. The reality is that poor parenting across all domains reviewed is at the heart of systematically delivering children into the hands of the criminal justice system.

Bibliography
The Research Supporting
The *5 Ugly Facts*

Introduction: The Set-Up

1.   The Sentencing Project. (2006). New incarceration figures: thirty-
        three consecutive years of growth. Retrieved August 31, 2008, from
        http://www.sentencingproject.org/Admin/Documents/publications
        /inc_newfigures.pdf

2.   Haney, W., Madaus, G., Abrams, L., Wheelock, A., Miao, J., & Gruia,
        I. (2004). The education pipeline in the United States: 1970 – 2000.
        Retrieved August 31, 2008, from http://www.bc.edu/research/
        nbetpp/statements/ nbr3.pdf

3.   Howell, J. (2003). Preventing and reducing juvenile delinquency: a
        comprehensive framework. Thousand Oaks, CA: Sage Publications.

4.   Diplomas count 2007: Ready for what? (2007). Education Week,
        26(40). Retrieved August 31, 2008, from
        http://www.edweek.org/ew/toc/2007/06/12/index.html

5.   Child Welfare Information Gateway. (2008). How the child welfare
        system works. Retrieved August 31, 2008, from
        http://www.childwelfare.gov/pubs/factsheets/ cpswork.cfm

6.   Coley, R.L., Lohman, B.J., Vortruba-Drzal, E., Pittman, L.D., &
        Chase-Lansdale, P.L. (2007). Maternal functioning, time, and money:
        the world of work and welfare. Child and Youth Services Review,
        29(6), 721-741. Retrieved August 31, 2008, from
        http://www.pubmedcentral.nih.gov/picrender.fcgi?tool=pmcentrez
        &artid=1948836&blobtype=pdf

7.   Bass, S., Shields, M.K., Behrman, R.E. (2004). Children, families, and
        foster care: analysis and recommendations. Children, Families, and
        Foster Care, 14(1), 5-29. Retrieved on August 31, 2008, from
        http://www.futureofchildren.org/information2826/information_sho
        w.htm?doc_id=209541

8.   Substance Abuse and Mental Health Services Administration
        (SAMHSA) & National Institutes of Health (NIH). (1999). Mental
        health: a report of the Surgeon General. Retrieved August 31, 2008,
        from http://www.surgeongeneral.gov/library/mentalhealth/
        home.html

9. Rounds-Bryant, J.L., Motivans, M. A., & Pelissier, B.M. (2004). Correlates of drug treatment outcomes for African American and white male federal prisoners: results from the TRIAD study. The American Journal of Drug and Alcohol Abuse, 30(3), 495-514.

10. United States Department of Justice, Bureau of Justice Statistics. (n.d.). The justice system: what is the sequence of events in the criminal justice system? Retrieved on August 31, 2008, from http://ojp.usdoj.gov/bjs/ justsys.htm#contents

11. Larson, D.B. & Johnson, B.R. (1998). Religion: the forgotten factor in cutting youth crime and saving at-risk urban youth. Retrieved August 31, 2008, from www.manhattan-institute.org/html/jpr-98-2.htm

12. The Barna Group (n.d.). Gender differences. Retrieved August 31, 2008, from http://www.barna.org/FlexPage.aspx?Page =Topic&TopicID=21

13. Copel, L.C. (2008). The lived experience of women in abusive relationships who sought spiritual guidance. Issues in Mental Health Nursing, 29(2), 115-130.

Ugly Fact #1
Education: Some Children
Are Deliberately Left Behind!

1. Haney, W., Madaus, G., Abrams, L., Wheelock, A., Miao, J., & Gruia, I. (2004). The education pipeline in the United States: 1970 – 2000. Retrieved August 31, 2008, from http://www.bc.edu/research/nbetpp/statements/ nbr3.pdf

2. Diplomas count 2007: Ready for what? (2007). Education Week, 26(40). Retrieved August 31, 2008, from http://www.edweek.org/ew/toc/2007/06/12/index.html

3. United States Department of Education. (2002). No Child Left Behind Act of 2001. Retrieved August 31, 2008, from http://www.ed.gov/policy/elsec/ leg/esea02/107-110.pdf

4. Gonzales, R., Richards, K., Seeley, K. (2002). Youth out of school: linking absence to delinquency. Denver, Colorado: Colorado Foundation for Families and Children. Retrieved August 31, 2008, from http://www.schoolengagement.org/TruancypreventionRegistry/Admin/Resources/Resources/YouthOutofSchoolLinkingAbsencetoDelinquency.pdf

5. Kober, N. (2001). It takes more than testing: Closing the achievement gap. A report of the Center on Education Policy. Washington, DC: Center on Education Policy. Retrieved August 31, 2008, from http://www.cepdc.org/index.cfm?fuseaction=document.showDocumentByID&DocumentID=137&varuniqueuserid=17779947666

6. United States Department of Education. (2007). Nations's report card. Retrieved August 31, 2008, from http://nationsreportcard.gov/ reading_math_grade12_2005/

7. Reynolds, AJ, Temple, JA, Robertson, DL, Mann, EA. (2001). Long-term effects of an early childhood intervention on educational achievement and juvenile arrest: a 15-year follow-up of low-income children in public schools. Journal of the American Medical Association, 285(18), 2339-46.

8.   Office of Educational Research and Improvement. (1992). Hard work and high expectations: motivating students to learn. Retrieved August 31, 2008, from http://www.kidsource.com/kidsource/content3/work.expectations.k12.4.html

9.   Cooper, CW. (2003). The detrimental impact of teacher bias: lessons learned from the standpoint of African American mothers. Teacher Education Quarterly. Retrieved August 31, 2008, from http://findarticles.com/p/articles/mi_qa3960/is_200304/ai_n9166548/pg_1?tag=artBody;col1

10.   Webster-Stratton C, Jamila Reid M, & Stoolmiller M. (2008). Preventing conduct problems and improving school readiness: evaluation of the Incredible Years Teacher and Child Training Programs in high-risk schools. Journal of Child Psychology and Psychiatry, 49(5), 471-488.

11.   Swanson, C.B. (2008). Cities in crisis: a special analytic report on high school. Retrieved August 31, 2008, from http://www.americaspromise.org/uploadedFiles/AmericasPromiseAlliance/Dropout_Crisis/SWANSONCitiesInCrisis040108.pdf

12.   Hanushek EA, & Rivkin SG. (2007). Pay, working conditions, and teacher quality. The Future of Children, 17(1), 69-86.

Ugly Fact #2
Child Welfare:
Helping *And* Hurting!

1.   Child Welfare Information Gateway. (2008). How the child welfare
        system works. Retrieved August 31, 2008, from
        http://www.childwelfare.gov/pubs/factsheets/cpswork.cfm

2.   Bass, S., Shields, M.K., Behrman, R.E. (2004). Children, families, and
        foster care: analysis and recommendations. Children, Families, and
        Foster Care, 14(1), 5-29. Retrieved August 31, 2008, from
        http://www.futureofchildren.org/information2826/information_sho
        w.htm?doc_id=209541

3.   Grabowski, LJS. (2006). It still don't make you feel like you doing it:
        welfare reform and perceived economic self-efficacy. Journal of
        Poverty, 10(3), 69-91. Retrieved on August 31, 2008, from
        http://www.pubmedcentral.nih.gov/picrender.fcgi?tool=pmcentrez
        &artid=1828031&blobtype=pdf

4.   Administration for Children and Families. (2007). TANF caseload
        data. Retrieved August 31, 2008, from http://www.acf.hhs.gov/
        programs/ofa/datareports/caseload/caseload_current.htm

5.   Administration for Children and Families. (2006). Characteristics and
        financial circumstances of TANF recipients FY 2006. Retrieved
        August 31, 2008, from http://www.acf.hhs.gov/programs/
        ofa/character/FY2006/indexfy06.htm

6.   Coley, R.L., Lohman, B.J., Vortruba-Drzal, E., Pittman, L.D., &
        Chase-Lansdale, P.L. (2007). Maternal functioning, time, and money:
        the world of work and welfare. Child and Youth Services Review,
        29(6), 721-741. Retrieved August 31, 2008, from
        http://www.pubmedcentral.nih.gov/picrender.fcgi?tool=pmcentrez
        &artid=1948836&blobtype=pdf

7.   Kober, N. (2001). It takes more than testing: Closing the
        achievement gap. A report of the Center on Education Policy.
        Washington, DC: Center on Education Policy. Retrieved August 31,
        2008, from http://www.cepdc.org/index.cfm?fuseaction=
        document.showDocumentByID&DocumentID=137&varuniqueuser
        id=17779947666

8.   US Department of Health and Human Services (2006). AFCARS
        report. Retrieved August 31, 2008, from http://www.acf.hhs.gov/
        programs/cb/stats_research/afcars/tar/report14.htm

9.   Harden, B.J. (2004). Safety and stability for foster care children: a
        developmental perspective. Children, Families, and Foster care, 14(1),
        Retrieved August 31, 2008, from http://www.futureofchildren.org/
        information2826/information_show.htm?doc_id=209543

10.   Rhodes-Courter, A. (2008). Three little words: a memoir. New York:
        Simon & Schuster, Inc.

11.   A critical look at the foster care system: foster care outcomes.
        Retrieved August 31, 2008, from http://www.liftingtheveil.org/
        foster14.htm

12.   Becker, D. R., Drake, R. E., & Naughton, W. J. Jr. (2005). Supported
        employment with co-occurring disorders. Psychiatric Rehabilitation
        Journal, 28, 332-338.

Ugly Fact #3
Mental Health:
Mental Illness Can Be Criminal!

1.	American Psychiatric Association. (2004). The Diagnostic and Statistical Manual of Mental Disorders, text-revised fourth edition. Washington, DC: American Psychiatric Association.

2.	Riolo, S.A., Nguyen, T.A., Greden, J.F., & King, C.A. (2005). Prevalence of depression by race/ethnicity: findings from the national health and nutrition examination survey III. American Journal of Public Health, 95(6), 998-1000. Retrieved August 31, 2008, from http://www.ajph.org/cgi/content/full/95/6/998

3.	National Survey on Drug Use and Health. (2008). Major depressive episodes among youths ages 12 -17. Retrieved August 31, 2008, from http://www.oas.samhsa.gov/highlights.htm

4.	National Institute on Mental Health (2004). The numbers count: mental disorders in America. Retrieved August 31, 2008, from http://www.nimh.nih.gov/health/publications/the-numbers-count-mental-disorders-in-america.shtml

5.	National Mental Health Information Center. (n.d.). Children's mental health facts: children and adolescents with anxiety disorders. Retrieved August 31, 2008, from http://mentalhealth.samhsa.gov/publications/allpubs/ca-0007/default.asp

6.	Substance Abuse and Mental Health Services Administration. (2007). Results from the 2006 National Survey on Drug Use and Health: National Findings (Office of Applied Studies, NSDUH Series H-32, DHHS Publication No. SMA 07-4293). Rockville, MD. Retrieved August 31, 2008, from http://www.oas.samhsa.gov/NSDUH/2k6NSDUH/2k6results.cfm#7.1.2

7.	Mental Health America (n.d.). Prevalence of mental disorders among children in the juvenile justice system. Retrieved August 31, 2008, from http://www1.nmha.org/children/justjuv/prevalence.cfm

8.   National Mental Health Information Center. (n.d.). Children's mental
        health facts: children and adolescents with attention
        deficit/hyperactivity disorder. Retrieved August 31, 2008, from
        http://mentalhealth.samhsa.gov/publications/allpubs/ca-
        0008/default.asp

9.   Substance Abuse and Mental Health Services Administration
        (SAMHSA) & National Institutes of Health (NIH). (1999). Mental
        health: a report of the Surgeon General. Retrieved August 31, 2008,
        from http://www.surgeongeneral.gov/library/mentalhealth/
        home.html

10.   National Alliance on Mental Illness. (n.d.). Mental health
        professionals: who they are and how to find one. Retrieved August
        31, 2008, from http://www.nami.org/Content/ContentGroups/
        Helpline1/Mental_Health_Professionals_Who_They_Are_and_How
        _to_Find_One.htm

11.   Taxman, F.S., Perdoni, M.L., & Harrison, L.D. (2007). Drug
        treatment services for adult offenders: the state of the state.
        Substance Abuse Treatment, 32(3), 239-254. Retrieved August 31,
        2008, from http://www.pubmedcentral.nih.gov/
        articlerender.fcgi?tool=pubmed&pubmedid=17383549

12.   Rounds-Bryant, J.L., & Baker, L. (2007). Substance dependence and
        level of treatment need among recently-incarcerated prisoners. The
        American Journal of Drug and Alcohol Abuse, 33, 1-5.

13.   United States Sentencing Commission (2007). Report to Congress:
        cocaine and federal sentencing policy. Retrieved August 31, 2008,
        from http://www.ussc.gov/r_congress/cocaine2007.pdf

14.   Hoffman, J., Fromke, S., & Cormier, M. (Producers). (2007).
        Addiction [Motion picture]. United States: Home Box Office.
        Retrieved August 31, 2008 from
        http://www.hbo.com/addiction/thefilm/

15.   Rounds-Bryant, J.L., Motivans, M. A., & Pelissier, B.M. (2004).
        Correlates of drug treatment outcomes for African American and
        white male federal prisoners: results from the TRIAD study. The
        American Journal of Drug and Alcohol Abuse, 30(3), 495-514.

Ugly Fact #4
Juvenile Justice:
Finishing School For Criminals!

1.   United States Department of Justice, Bureau of Justice Statistics. (n.d.). The Justice System: What is the sequence of events in the criminal justice system? Retrieved on August 31, 2008, from http://ojp.usdoj.gov/bjs/justsys.htm#contents

2.   Real Police. (n.d.). Police history. Retrieved August 31, 2008, from http://www.realpolice.net/police-history.shtml

3.   United States Department of State. (2004). Outline of the U.S. legal system. Retrieved August 31, 2008, from http://usinfo.state.gov/products/pubs/legalotln/criminal.htm

4.   PBS. (n.d.). Child or adult: a century-long view. Retrieve August 31, 2008, from http://www.pbs.org/wgbh/pages/frontline/shows/ juvenile/stats/childadult.html

5.   Howell, J. (2003). Preventing and reducing juvenile delinquency: a comprehensive framework. Thousand Oaks, CA: Sage Publications.

6.   Deconto, J., Chambers, S.B., & Spies, S. (2008, March 13). Suspects' probation oversight questioned. Raleigh News & Observer. Retrieved August 31, 2008, from http://www.newsobserver.com/ 2811/story/998319.html

7.   Dees, M. (2008, March 13). Lovette held, freed repeatedly. Raleigh News & Observer. Retrieved August 31, 2008, from http://www.newsobserver.com/2811/story/1081301.html

Ugly Fact #5
Faith Community:
Breeding Ground for Juvenile Delinquency!

1. Larson, D.B. & Johnson, B.R. (1998). Religion: the forgotten factor in cutting youth crime and saving at-risk urban youth. Retrieved August 31, 2008, from http://www.manhattan-institute.org/html/jpr-98-2.htm

2. Blank, M.B., Mahmood, M.M., Fox, J.C., Guterbock, T. (2002). Alternative mental health services: the role of the black church. American Journal of Public Health, 92(10), 1668-1672.

3. The Barna Group (n.d.). Gender differences. Retrieved August 31, 2008, from http://www.barna.org/FlexPage.aspx?Page=Topic&TopicID=21

4. Levitt, H.M., & Ware, K. (2006). Anything with two heads is a monster: religious leaders' perspective on marital equality and domestic violence. Violence Against Women, 12(12), 1169-90.

5. Texas Health and Human Services Commission. (2006). The faith community and domestic violence. Retrieved August 31, 2008, from http://www.hhsc.state.tx.us/programs/familyviolence/HHSC_Clergy_English.pdf

6. Howell, J. (2003). Preventing and reducing juvenile delinquency: a comprehensive framework. Thousand Oaks, CA: Sage Publications.

7. Rounds-Bryant, J.L. (2007). Domestic violence is an equal opportunity killer. In Men don't like kids: 5 ugly facts about human behavior (pp. 73-92). Durham, NC: Mental Health Solutions. Retrieved August 31, 2008, from http://www.5uglyfacts.com

8. Copel, L.C. (2008). The lived experience of women in abusive relationships who sought spiritual guidance. Issues in Mental Health Nursing, 29(2), 115-130.

9. Administration for Children and Families. (2008). Summary: child maltreatment 2006. Retrieved August 31, 2008, from http://www.acf.hhs.gov/programs/cb/pubs/cm06/summary.htm

10.   Briere, J., & Elliott, D.M. (2003). Prevalence and psychological sequelae of self-reported childhood physical and sexual abuse in a general population sample of men and women. Child Abuse & Neglect, 27(10), 1205-1222.

11.   Socolar, R.R., Cabinum-Foeller, E., & Sinal, S.H. (2008). Is religiosity associated with corporal punishment or child abuse? Southern Medical Journal, 101(7), 707-710.

12.   Wolfe, D.A., Francis, K.J., & Straatman, A.L. (2006). Child abuse in religiously-affiliated institutions: long-term impact on men's mental health. Child Abuse & Neglect, 30(2), 205-212.

13.   Fortune, M. (1991). A commentary on religious issues in family violence. In Violence in the family: a workshop curriculum for clergy and other helpers (pp. 137-151). Cleveland: The Pilgrim Press. Retrieved August 31, 2008, from http://new.vawnet.org/ Assoc_Files_VAWnet/ReligiousIssues.pdf

14.   The National Center for the Victims of Crime. (n.d.). Child sexual abuse. Retrieved August 31, 2008, from http://www.ncvc.org/ncvc/ main.aspx?dbName=DocumentViewer&DocumentID=32315

15.   Dale, K.A., & Alpert, J.L. (2007). Hiding behind the cloth: child sexual abuse and the Catholic Church. Journal of Child Sexual Abuse, 16(3), 59-74.

16.   Worley, K.B., & Church, J.K. (2007). When children sexually abuse other children. The Journal of the Arkansas Medical Society, 103 (8), 205-208.

17.   The Barna Group. (2007). The spirituality of moms outpaces that of dads. Retrieved August 31, 2008, from http://www.barna.org/ FlexPage.aspx?Page=BarnaUpdate&BarnaUpdateID=270

18.   Podles, L.P. (1993). Men and religion. Touchstone, 6(2). Retrieved August 31, 2008, from http://www.touchstonemag.com/ archives/article.php?id=06-02-014-f

Book Orders

Titles of Books:
Men Don't Like Kids!　　　　　　　　_____

It Takes A Village To Raise A Criminal!　　_____

Number of Books: _____ x $24.95 =　　_____
Tax (6.75% for NC residents only):　　　_____

Shipping: *(Free)*:　　　　　　　　　_____

Total Amount of Order:　　　　　　　_____

Shipping Information (Please Print Clearly!)

Name: _____

Shipping Address:_____

City/State/Zip Code: _____

Telephone Number: _____

Payment Information

Please make checks and money orders payable to **MHS**

Mailing Address

Mail payment and order form to: Mental Health Solutions, P.O. Box 14413, Research Triangle Park, NC 27709-4413.

Book Orders for
Men Don't Like Kids!
It Takes A Village To Raise A Criminal!

Copies of *5 Ugly Facts* are available at discount for bulk purchases, including fund-raising. The books are ideal for basic training in public service, human service, religious, and social organizations. Find more details about placing orders at
www.5UglyFacts.com

Speaking Engagements
Contact Dr. Jennifer L. Rounds-Bryant at
drjenn@5UglyFacts.com